Knees of a Natural Man

The Selected Poetry of Henry Dumas

Edited and with an Introduction by Eugene B. Redmond

NEW YORK

Published in the United States by Thunder's Mouth Press
54 Greene Street, Suite 4S, New York, N.Y. 10013

Library of Congress Cataloging-in-Publication Data:

Dumas, Henry, 1934–1968
     Knees of a natural man: poetry / by Henry Dumas.
        p.   cm.
     ISBN 0-938410-75-X: $19.95
     ISBN 0-938410-74-1 (pbk.): $9.95
     I. Title.
PS3554.U43K6   1989
811'.54—dc19   88-38377
                                                                      CIP

Grateful acknowledgment is made to the New York State Council on the Arts and
the National Endowment for the Arts for their financial assistance in the publication
of this work.

The persons and events depicted in this work are fictitious. Any resemblance to
actual persons or events is purely coincidental.

Designed by Clare Ultimo, Inc.

Printed in the United States of America

Distributed by
Consortium Book Sales and Distribution, Inc.
213 East 4th Street, St. Paul, MN 55101

The extended Dumas family wishes to express our sincere gratitude and appreciation to Eugene Redmond, who has been his brother's keeper, who has carried the work, whose sense of poetry is even more than poems.

Contents

A Natural Man

Where the Sidewalk Ends

Blues Songs

Listen to the Sound of My Horn!

Thoughts/Images

Kef (Selections)

FIRST SERIES

Ikefs (Ikons of Kef)

Saba (Selections)

Songthesis: East St. Louis Epiphanies

Introduction

Poet Henry Dumas:
Distance Runner, Stabilizer, Distiller

"Music and I have come at last!"
—Henry Dumas

He came out of the vast *somewhere*—like the music—with the music, mounting Robert Hayden's "rocking loom of history."
He was tuned in. Turned on. Cultural stabilizer. Cultural modulator. Funkadelic verb-gymnast. Irreversibly switched to Everyblood.

And, like his Everyblood counterpart in that oft-sung scroll *Ark of Bones*, Henry Lee Dumas (1934-1968) was *called* to bear witness to the terrible swish and sass and swoon of life; to bear and *bare* the word. To shuttle the word between its far/near distances and its points of distillation along the Blackhuman Continuum. Wordwise he was sent to honor and *re*-illuminate those ancient things that remain in the ears. To sculpt slavery into song and churn commotion into poetry.

The word was Henry Dumas's Way. Shape. Form. Fashion. *Rite* was his other middle name. Having been *called*, he became the *caller*. We also name him—thanks to Otis Williams—*Bluesician*. Since, to paraphrase Conrad Kent Rivers, he moved through the many-tiered channels and straits of our world as those channels and straits moved through him. Homeboy, from Sweet Home, he tailored dire poems and songs for dire straits. Nor, he was to whisper in "Rose Jungle," would he "lesson their love."

Virtually unknown beyond Black Arts and little magazine communities at the time of his violent death in 1968, Dumas, as viewed by Imamu Amiri Baraka, was, "an underground deity, glowing into ascension into post-material recognition." And now, "after the death of his body," we have, in *Knees of a Natural Man*, "his mystical insistence." Insisting. Persisting. Perpetual. Like earth. Like life. Like Africa. Like wordworlds. Baraka, who prefaced the Southern Illinois University edition of *Poetry for My People*, had known Henry Dumas and published him in *Black Fire*. "The [Dumas] spirit glows," Baraka gleaned, "speaking in his curious tongue. The ancient black language." Add to this *a musico-graphic alphabet*—and then, "Listen to the Sound of My Horn!"

He lived in the breach, in the stretch; "Henry Dumas lived very rapidly, and very slowly," according to Jay Wright in that Baraka-prefaced volume of Dumas's poetry. "We could never seem to keep up with him, or catch him, or hold him when we did . . . There was simply so very much to do." His wife, Loretta Dumas, attests that: "Henry seemed to be awake even when he was asleep." Clyde Taylor, who makes several masterful analyses in "Henry Dumas: Legacy of a Long-Breath Singer," offers this:

> The city as background to his people is rendered in a fantastical, opaque, sketchy way, insanely electric and as absurd as his own subterranean death . . . [Consequently,] The reader faces relief when he passes from one world to another at the place "where the sidewalk ends" and zebras spring from the imagination into reality.

He was a "natural" man—in the fullest, lightest, brightest, blackest, yet most complex, sense of that word—and by turns playful, brooding-moody, contemplative, histrionic, introspective, gregarious, handsome, solemn, proud, scornful, impatient with a sluggish consciousness, weird, way out, outlandish, meditative, loving, in love, out of love, lofty, perspicacious, unkempt, meticulous, studied, paranoid, potent, impotent, deep, indulgent, verbally dexterous, mum, angry, altruistic, heroic, discombobulated, and high, always, high on language. Such were the emotional streams and reaches that tortured and tempered Henry Dumas. Though *whole*, he was never *one* thing or person. Instead, he was multitudinous. And, in some ways, sacrificial.

Osiris. Osiris. He was an ancient African god and culture hero, Osiris, whose "spirit" wings and "broods over Henry Dumas and suffuses his generation." Such is the frame-view of Stephen Henderson. Myth and man, Dumas is, Henderson says, the "prototype of the New Man, griot, seer, shaman, Homeboy, Ace, Brother, poet." He hooked his cultural-natal cord onto the line of the African Continuum and parachuted into the Babel of life. Henderson, himself a caller, acknowledges:

> I call him Osiris. Emmett Till. Orpheus. Malcolm. King. Bird. Coltrane. George Jackson. Medgar Evers. I call him Robert Johnson. Stackolee. Railroad Bill. He was metonymy

and metaphor. A megaphone. A magna vox. A master
blaster. A signifier. A signified. Item: small black boy in
bloody fetal curl. Item: Jimmy Powell wasted in his prime.
The sweet voice from Sweet Home. The ancient voice.
The protospeech. The metalanguage. Linguist of the soul.
Poetry as time warp. Galactic intertextuality. Descent into
Hell. Into self. Music of the blood. Music of the stars.

Intoxicated by language, Dumas existed in the twain, the twixt,
the sundown, the daybreak, the twilight zone. Poetic madness,
that renowned stance of perpetual creative edginess, was his to em-
brace. As he said, he was, in this heady suspension, low and be-
low, high and up high. Music, the rhythmization of vision and
adventure, was his vehicular ode for traversing the Soular System.
An experimental conveyer belt being fast-forwarded and re-wound
simultaneously, musicalized language and sight (Jay Wright's
"rhythm of perception") helped Dumas synthesize and balance
him*selves* in the driving whir-blur of daily commotion. It helped
him re-quiet fears and dangers induced by swollen passions, pres-
sures, obsessions, racism, and abuse of spirit.

A day in the life of Henry Dumas, Poet, was like a week or
month in the life of the average—and not so average—person. All
observers made note of his unabashed thirst-quest for sacred-secret
knowledge, his pithy third-eye descent or ascent into an off-limits
regions of the Soular System and his cross-dimensional flights to
edges, ledges and perches from which there appeared to be no re-
turn. He moved through the world as the world moved through
him. Deep channel fisherman. Asides. Marginalia. Between lines.
Between thighs. Linear. Cyclical. Rites. Baby-making. Fingerer of
the multicultural keys. *Play Ebony Play Ivory.* Footnotes.
Thoughts/Images. Like Richard Wright, whose work he mastered,
Dumas chose to write "imaginatively" out of his own "experi-
ences": Sweet Home, that sweet-sour womb-cradle in the midst of
a deranged (and mis-arranged) Southland. "Mosaic Harlem," that
UpSouth sanctuary, where real life is rendered as a "Montage":

> . . . the street walked in front
> of me and by lamp eyes the people
> grew up like stone thoughts
> cemented to the height of the
> steel sky . . .

Montage, yes, with its metal echoes of Claude McKay's refrain:
America as a "cultured hell."

The lengthening totem of Dumas's own montage? Commerce High School. Boy Scouts. Photography. Poetry. Streams of lyrical fractions from a bottomless and uninhibited boy-man. Fiction. Cultural shards. City College in New York. Four years in the U.S. Air Force. One year in the Arabian Peninsula. Marriage. Two sons. Rutgers University. Civil Rights. Tent Cities. Black Arts/Black Movement. African Continuum. Yoroba Priests. Malcolm Gone. King Gone. Coltrane Gone. Gone. Gone. Gone. Like he was too soon to be—Gone—in a New York City subway shooting drama of "unclarified" origins. Hiram College. Southern Illinois University's Experiment in Higher Education. East St. Louis. Little Magazines: *Untitled, Camel, American Weave, Negro Digest, Hiram Poetry Review, Collection, Freedomways.* Cultural heroes: Sun Ra. James Brown. Blues-begetting-Blues. Moms Mabley. Paul Robeson. Langston Hughes. Gospel. Mahalia. Léopold Sédar Senghor. Otis Redding as in "Owed to Otis."

Arriving in East St. Louis in the summer of 1967 was another "natural" ("high") for Henry Dumas. He met Katherine Dunham. Clyde C. Jordan. Taylor Jones, III. The Black Egyptians. Joseph E. Harrison. Imperial War Lords. Hordes of students, new fans, street-corner liberators. Revolution aborning, Black Arts aborning, Love aborning, East Boogie yelling-moaning/first-born-like under the healthy strain of the New Black Consciousness and Renaissance II. At the Experiment in Higher Education, where he joined Oliver Jackson, Joyce Ladner, and Edward Crosby, he poured all his lives into the horn through which he blew sweet-sour sermons of Trane, Sun Ra, Ogotemmeli, Jomo Kenyatta, Shakespeare, Geronimo, Malcolm, Ralph Ellison, Margaret Walker, James Weldon Johnson, Kenneth Clarke, Alexander Calder, Socrates, Bo Didley, Sojourner, Fannie Lou Hamer, *The Jesus Bag, Black Voices* . . . the sermons and the rites went on. His favorite poems at East St. Louis readings were "Ngoma," "America," "Island Within Island," "The Puppets Have a New King," "Black Star Line," "Hunt" and "Son of Msippi."

Slugs. The East. Celebrity Room. Naomi's Restaurant. Teacher-Counselor scrimmages. Sherman Fowler. Clem Fiori. Earl Thomas. John "Bird" Brooks. *For Malcolm X.* And "Epiphany," a lance-poem born out of night-mooded conversations, testy warrior rap, beer-lunches and sexual tease. "Take off your clothes," was the much-heard challenge around the Experiment in Higher Education in East St. Louis. I used the phrase frequently as did Dumas and other members of our literary-activist cult. However, some faculty members and residents, gleaning only the surface-literal meaning, were uncomfortable with its use. So Dumas, who already had innumerable references to "naked" in his poems and stories, wrote "Epiphany" and dedicated it to me. It was both a private, brotherly statement, and a mythic-mystical trip.

> A man runs out into a field.
> The sun is shining arrows.
> The rivers of the earth
> converge and fan out from
> his feet and the mountains
> east of the moon and west
> of everything else
> grow beneath his feet
> and all the clothed
> and feathered birds
> watch him from the road
> and the man takes off
> joyously all
> his clothes!

Thus Dumas, the supreme celebrant, metaphorically explained that comic-serious phrase which had embarrassed some and naughtily delighted others. Running man seeks "natural" light and clothing which he will witness for the living, the dead and the yet-to-be-born. His search intersects his additional quest for identity, i.e., psychological direction and truth, and Soular nutrition for the whole BEing (family). To obtain these nutrients, he must spiritually and poetically connect with cosmic rhythm, cosmic energy and the cosmological continuum. Hence, "Epiphany" is a fertility ritual of cultural reclamation, tribal regeneration, creative fecundity and human-natural kinship. It represented a master poet and griot saluting a brother-bard, a new friend to whom Dumas frequently referred as a "writin nigger", which was something I had not experienced until then—that is, an accomplished Black writer telling me that I could write well. And then to have two poems—"Owed to Otis" and "Epiphany"—inspired by me! How much more can a so-help-me-John Henry-hope-to-die poet expect in one live-time?

Like Ellison, Henry Dumas went to the territory, taking territory and testament with him. As his former student, poet Sherman Fowler announces: "Africa is not just a place; Africa is wherever Africans live or hunt or die." Hence Africanized physiques, thinking and ritual became central to Dumas's daily thrust—his libidinal engine fueled by songified strageties for survival. (Stephen Henderson's "survival motion.") *The Prevalence of*

Ritual follows from this thinking: evident, evidenced, witnessed. Through the cultural vessel-poet, life is songified, rarified, ritualized and lush. Dumas's major poems reflect his debt, his subservience, to the All-One; to, then, the Oneness of Being: The Big Black Faith-Rock. Hence Fluidity. Inclusion. Dexterity. No predictable tone; no formal, graduate writing school, "closure." Rather, he is the keys and chords in *Play Ebony Play Ivory;* "us," "my people" and "eagles" in "The Coming of the Eagles"; one-with-the-winds and the *word-behind-the-word* in "Emoyeni, Place of the Winds"—where

> it is time to make the time

in Zululand, in Sweet Home, in Windy City, in Watts, in Harlemland, in East St. Louis, because *Emoyeni Emoyeni* sweeping across the "tongue of zulus," means, if anything, that

> it is my father singing
> it is my mother at the river
> it is the spear and the chain
> it is time to swallow the hill[.]

As the immersed warrior-poet hears

> emoyeni going going

he is also co-conspirator to its regenerative and redemptive aftermath:

> I see the coming of the long green rain[.]

"Ngoma" and "Black Star Line" continue Dumas's fascination with the roots of Black Culture, which he potion-packed with a mine-field-of-an imagination and stunning creative power. The word as act, way, shape, form, fashion. As in "Ngoma" which I heard him read to students at Southern Illinois University in 1967. In this poem, and in "Black Star Line," he stretches out—gets raw, does it "Straight, No Chaser." Call and Response. Gyral. Visceral. Sexual. Ritual. Syncopation. Sanctified. Sumptuous. Sacred. Secular. Feeling Through. Swahili. Zulu. Afrocentric. Bibliocentric. Grand Classical. Funky. Fidgety. Anxious. Antiphony. Its high-lows—*aiwa* aiwa—and searchingly deep/ritualistic reaches recall for me a statement by Ugandan poet Okot p'Bitek: "To fully understand this poem you need 10,000 dancers on the shore!" Celebration. Dumas would have loved Kool and the Gang. Earth Wind and Fire. The Gap Band. Like he loved James Brown, Otis Redding, Wilson Pickett, Della and Elmore James. As we say in the bush, *he liked that kind of carrying on.* "Ngoma"—"drum" in Swahili and "song" in Zulu—is Fingers playing upon drumskin and foreskin and belly. Ears to belly to boom-sound beating. Yes, the drum resonates at the center of Dumas's Soular System.

Songifying and sashaying his way toward "Black Star Line," Dumas disembarks at "Coat of Many Fibers" with its "white cotton" and those "black and brown/fingers picking it." Once Europe has been "carved" upon them, the "Puppets" create a new African-Diasporan song, laced with slavery, old-time religion and Eurocentric solemnity. How they work, what they made, is reminiscent of James Weldon Johnson's "O Black and Unknown Bards". The mobile history of song is charted. For in "Coat of Many Fibers," Puppets merge with "kerosene-lighted/shadows" and:

> With a line of blood,
> a thread of weeping and moaning,
> a strain of song,
> a streak of tears,
> and a grasp of the white fiber,
> the fingers spun a hymn to God.

Origins: Shouts. Work Songs. Fables. Spirituals. Blues. Jazz. Rhythm 'n Blues. Soul. Rap. Henry Dumas.
Everyblood resurfaces in "Msippi" where:

> (Bare walk and cane stalk
> make a hungry belly talk.)

and "the river of death" doubles as "the river of pain," (recording like a watery tape, the history of pain!), seen slithering, "muscling" along the "long red earth dipping, rising/spreading out in deltas and plains." This "Msippi" ("Sippi") drips with "moss and snakes" where the narrator/conductor "grew/up" on the pain-stained-blues "wailing" of:

> Woman gone woe man too
> baby cry rent-pause daddy flew.

Jay Wright informed us that Dumas was "searching" for a poetic "Structure" that was "analogous" to "music". Yes. Multi-leveled, multi-talented, multi-angled, multi-cultural and multi-lingual,

Dumas nevertheless spun his many-fibered predicament (DuBois's "veil") around an Afrocentric cultural encasement. Protector, pioneer, pilot and participant that he was. It was not easy, Clyde Taylor reminds us, for this young and genius-angered Black man to idea-sync the cultural, aesthetic, sexual, economic, racial and political commotion that perpetually stalked him. But, as all observers admit, he was working hard at it. As he extended and redefined his vision, he harkened back to truths and mysteries that gave rise to the First World. To First Rhyme. To First Man and First Woman: *mwanamume* and *mume* and *mwali*.

"Black Star Line," like "Ngoma" in another sphere of the Soular System, represents Dumas's attempt to salve and balm "the Jesus disease" and other New World maladies. Clyde Taylor observed that:

> Dumas aspired to the oldest, most honored version of poet/prophet to his people. He sought to incarnate their cultural identity, values, and mythic visions as well as codify and even reshape those myths into modalities of a more soulful existence. . . . The miracle of Dumas' work, worth the name *genius*, is that he had already integrated the formidable demands of this role when the new concept of Black writing was just emerging. His poetry, particularly, represents an extension of the role of communal seer in ways that anticipate, comment on, exemplify, and sometimes sharply diverge from more popular versions of the new writing.

Indeed, like Whitman, Dumas was one with the All-Body, one with Everyblood. Hence in "Black Star Line," "black mothers" are "singing" and "black fathers" are "chanting". At once a poetic and history-studded homage to his hero Marcus Mosiah Garvey and a gift of tongues to his own people, "Black Star Line," like Langston Hughes' "The Negro Speaks of Rivers," evokes thousands of years of Black Civilization. "Ngoma" intones that underneath all the polyrhythms and the contrapuntal bleats lies a monumental order, harmony, grand scheme of coordination. It says the Soular System backs us up. "Black Star Line" draws the map—charts the course via poetic footwork—to those sources. "Black mothers" sing:

> Sons, my sons,
> dip into this river with your ebony cups
> A vessel of knowledge sails under power.
> Study stars as well as currents.
> Dip into this river with your ebony cups.

It seeps deep, as the 1960s poets used to say. And, as testimony to that depth, "Black Star Line" is the premiere Afrocentric poetic scroll, Dumas's philosophical-cultural update of Richard Wright's "Blueprint for Negro Writing"—rendered a quarter of a century later during the fabled and fabulous Renaissance II. In "Blues Songs" Dumas songified and signified about "surface" acceptances and how machines were being readied to replace human functions. "Black Star Line" cautions "Sons, my sons" against being shallow, derelict, uncommitted, ambivalent, insensitive, and cowardly, in the struggle for freedom and liberation. The poem is a libation, in fact, for liberation. "Black fathers" are "chanting":

> Send cargoes and warriors back to sea.
> Remember the pirates and their chains of nails.
> Let ebony strike the blow that launches this ship.
> Make your heads not idle sails, blown about
> by any icy wind like a torn page from a book.

Like Hughes, Dumas sought spiritually and culturally to unite his Black World ("all you golden-black children of the sun"); he recalled the past, which can only be reconstructed and re-entered by dispossessed people if they "make heavy-boned ships that break a wave and pass it." Then, and only then, can they "Bring back sagas from Songhay, Kongo, Kaaba,/deeds and works of Malik, Toussaint, Marcus,/statues of Mahdi and a lance of lightning." Black mothers, finally, anoint "sons" with birth-*rites:*

> Children of my flesh,
> dip into this river with your ebony cups.
> A ship of knowledge sails unto wisdom

Moving through this world as the world moved through him, Dumas gathered much about world literatures, religions, philosophies, languages, peoples, cultures, ways, manners, customs and feelings. He experimented to no-end, nothing ever ended for him, eyeing, as he *moved*, every tangible and intangible thing-being as a potential brother-sojourner through his Soular System.
Knees of a Natural Man takes:

> me and my ole man . . . to the fulton fish market[.]

There

> we walk around in the guts and the scales

and later,

> we scaling on our knees back uptown on lenox[.]

One of Dumas's recurring lecture themes was taken from the "text"/stanza of "Ikef 9: Black Widow":

> And who sent the
> nigger wandering in
> the night?

This pain of uprootedness, poetically recalled in "The Puppets Have a New King," had produced, in Dumas's mind, another wasteful symptom, which he restated often, as in "Ikef 13":

> When will we cease
> bowing?

　In both his poetic/astral and "natural" lives, Dumas worshipped children ("of the sun"), none more than his own sons—David and Michael—and so he could write the child-man poem, "My little Boy":

> My little boy speaks
> with an accent.
> I must remember sometime
> to lean my head down
> and whisper in his ear
> and ask him the name
> of the country
> he comes from.
> I like his accent.

　Much humor. Much seriousness. Much love. Much Sex. Big fun: "If You Behave," "I Laugh Talk Joke," "The Buster," "Grandma's Got a Brand New Wig," "Too Hot to Handle Blues," "Kef 2," "Kef 25," "Saba: Joy," "Peas" and the brightly ticklish "Yams":

> I made a yamship for my belly with my spoon
> and sweet riding jelly bread kept me til noon.

Or he waxes, with Countee Cullen, heritage-wise; but without the heavy strain (and string) of competing selves, as in "Funk":

The great god Shango in the African sea
reached down with palm oil and oozed out me.

Dumas's work is deceptively effortless in places. The appearance
of spontaneity and improvisation was the result of long hours of
meditation in the deep channels of etymology, musicology, re-
ligion, philosophy, linguistics, and self-investigation. So when he
flips one of those wit-laced lyrical morsels over his shoulders at you
beware and savor it substantively. Even check out the menus. Ditto
for "Listen to the Sound of My Horn!" *(can't you hear it in your
bones?)* and "Songthesis: East St. Louis Epiphonies" where you
hear/see/feel . . .

> brown sound chocolate
> memories
> like the first time
> you saw grapes
> and tasted them
> and learned the color
> blue

Heights. He was a tasty/testy poet of Heights. Salutes. Sorcery.
Sensuality. Non-Sensical. He remained intoxicated by the lan-
guage all his days. And nights. *Saba:* an ancient kingdom, literal
and figurative, and future golden-stool of those on whom the
proverbial "hurt" has been put. *Saba:* acknowledgement of the
anointed, the appointed, the chosen who ("Kef 40") "have a jour-
ney/to take and little time"; and who "have ships to name and
crews." *Saba:* the ancient scroll-legend, cloth-robes, place-kingdom
in Saudi Arabia. And *Kef*—the ancient ecstatic state of Jazz-
High—with its *Ikons* that keep eye over those over-anesthetized by
language, lore and trance. By something being "put" on you. By
hoochie-coochie, mojo, djuka, juju and Holy Roller Hums. Part of
Dumas's being perpetually aspired to other elevations. (Hear K.
Curtis Lyle's "Unexpected Elevations.") Most great poets have
been thus driven, thus smitten, thus rushed, thus loving, thus
needful, thus enslaved by tongue-spells. The higher the high
("Owed to Otis"), the purer, the rawer, the funkier the sound. And
to be sure, Dumas gyrated, rite-worded in the Cosmic Funk Shop.

For Dumas, song, songified language, spiritual depth, psycho-
logical balance and cultural self-knowledge were the most potent
forces in the Soular System. He wrote out of countless bags on
innumerable subjects. But, without subtracting from his loft of cre-

ative achievement, it must be known that the power-ideas which drove him most profoundly were those closest to his ethnographical and cultural core. He could *think* Black, if you will, without cluttering his cosmic view with petty, cheap, narrow, chauvinistic and sub-sensitive chaff.

"A Black poet can praise the sun, too!" he exclaimed during a lecture at SIU-EHE, adding that "A Black poet is a preacher." And so, like primeval bards prancing at their primeval stations, he was a "natural" man, playing ebony/playing ivory, and pledging "Greatness":

> each man
> a string on the harp
> doing its own destiny
> no one pushing
> no one behind
> each man
> the end
> and the beginning
> of harmony.

Poetic cuisine for the hungry, hounding ages. Even now, from his pioneer's perch, he beacons and beckons those of us who quest, who sing, who surge, as it were, on our ritual march through his and our own Soular System—and Renaissance III.

Eugene B. Redmond
December 1, 1988
East St. Louis, Illinois

Acknowledgements

The good struggle to perpetuate the "Henry Dumas Movement"—as Jayne Cortez calls it—began in May of 1968 as his grief-borne family, friends, and colleagues sought to assemble the foggy details of his bizarre and sudden death and prepare the most fitting vehicles by which his brilliantly original creations should be conveyed to the wider world. Toward such ends, practically every conceivable approach, medium, technique or forum has been pressed into service. Consequently, the bearers of the Dumas Scrolls now form so vast a weave of cults and extended families that naming them here would be next to impossible. Some, however, must be recited: Edward Crosby, Donald Henderson, Hale Chatfield, the late John S. Rendleman, the late Joseph E. Harrison, Ronald Tibbs, Sons/Ancestors Players of Sacramento, Toni Morrison, Quincy Troupe, Rosalind Goddard, Clyde Taylor, Tommy Ellis, the late Walter Lowenfels, Oliver Jackson, Maya Angelou, George A. Jones/Ahaji Umbudi, Vernon T. Hornback, T. Michael Gates, Keith Aytch, Raymond Patterson, Imamu Amiri Baraka, Marie Brown, Jay Wright, Margaret Walker Alexander, Lincoln T. Beauchamp, William Halsey, Anthony Sloan, Avery Brooks, the late Hoyt Fuller, Val Grey Ward/Kuumba, Sterling Plumpp, H. Mark Williams/Cultural Messengers, the late Larry Neal, and my delightfully literate editorial assistant Lori Reed. Since 1985, I have been adjusting to my reentry into East St. Louis, where, among other things, a Eugene B. Redmond Writers Club has been formed. It is one of the staunchest champions of the Henry Dumas Movement, and its members—especially Sherman Fowler, Darlene Roy, Evon Udoh, Frank Nave and Cheryl Byers—have been at the local forefront of the struggle. Finally, I'd like to pay homage to the indefatigable and faith-filled Loretta Dumas, who lives with her son, Michael, in Somerset, New Jersey, and who maintains an admirable courage and dignity through all the "falls and rises" of the Movement.

—E.B.R.

Play Ebony,
Play Ivory

Play Ebony Play Ivory

    play ebony play ivory
play chords that
    speak primeval
    play ebony play ivory
play notes that
    speak my people ...

    play ebony play ivory
play til air explodes
play til it subsides
    play ebony play ivory.

for the songless, the dead
who rot the earth
all these dead,
whose muted sour tongues
speak broken chords,
all these aging people
poison the heart of earth.

they cannot sing
they cannot play
they cannot breathe the early rhythm
they never heard the pulse of womb

so up! you bursting lungs
you spirits of morning breath
up! and make fingers

3

and play long and play soft
    play ebony play ivory.

play my people
all my people who breathe
the breath of earth
all my people who are keys and chords . . .

now touch
and hear and see
let your lungs scream
til they explode
til blood subsides
and flesh vibrates . . .

make chords that speak
play long play soft
    play ebony play ivory
    play ebony
    play ivory

The Coming of the Eagles

Let us have eagles!
Let us have eagles
among my people!

The hot wind has melted
ice and the ice has fallen.
The cold wind has chiseled mountains
and they have fallen.
The dry wind has gnawed

4

away stone and stone is sand.
The cruel winds have cut
feathers, skin and bone,
and the sparrows have died.

Let us have new wings
among my people!
Let us have bones
among my people!
Let us have visions
among my people!

Let us ride the wind
into the high country.
Let us have eagles!

Rite

Vodu green clinching his waist,
obi purple ringing his neck,
Shango, God of the spirits,
whispering in his ear,
thunderlight stabbing the island
of blood rising from his skull.

Mojo bone in his fist
strikes the sun from his eye.
Iron claw makes his wrist.
He recalls the rites of strength
carved upon his chest.
Black flame, like tongues of glass,
ripples beneath a river of sweat.

Strike the island!
Strike the sun!
Strike the eye of evil!
Strike the guilty one!

No power can stay the mojo
when the obi is purple
and the vodu is green
and Shango is whispering,
Bathe me in blood.
I am not clean.

Hunt

antelope falls
i watch
jakqula cut
i watch
titio cut
i watch
yakub lift
i watch
all carry
i leg beneath
i tongue
falling blood
i am butang
dog

Emoyeni, Place of the Winds

Emoyeni, passing passing
from the tongue of the zulus
comes this word
Emoyeni place of the winds

you come
we will climb the body of the hill
thru the bowing of the talking grass
up the footpath where the spirits pass

look, emoyeni passing rising
by the crumbling rock and the fingerreeds
I put my ear to the mouth of an old man
Emoyeni passing passing, is what he told me

Listen to the wind, my son
see the coming of its children
every nation leans down to bite the hill
passing blowing emoyeni place of the winds

come
it is time to make the time
I see with my skin and hear with my tongue
emoyeni from the sky
emoyeni the tongue of many years passing
where the fingers from the earth rising
stroke all the singers passing passing
by the rumbling of the falling rock
down the valleys of the congo leaping
toward the body of the hill

breathe
it is time to make the time

it is my father singing
it is my mother at the river
it is the spear and the chain
it is your time to swallow the hill
breathe
emoyeni passing passing
behind the dust
emoyeni passing passing
behind the fear
emoyeni going going
I see the coming of the long green rain

Ngoma

ngoma*
put thine ear to my belly O *mwanamume*
    who is my husband
put thine ear here
listen the boom-sound beating there
put thy head over closer O *mume*
    who is my lover
feel this chest-sound pounding
    in thine ear's drum
    aiwa aiwa
it is the chest-sound
same that booms my chest
    aiwa aiwa
a strong sound running
like feet of gazelle
    aiwa aiwa
O mwali who is my wife

* "*Ngoma*" means "drum" in Swahili. [H. D.]

8

put thy fingers here O *mume*
      who knows my skin
feel the skin-sound singing there

      aiwa aiwa
      thy belly sings
      thy belly dances
      aiwa aiwa
      my fingers dance
      my fingers sing
      louder sings the boom-sound louder
      the spirit chants the child-sound's name
      aiwa aiwa O *mwali* in my morning
      mother of beauty mother of sun
      listen O my woman
      spirits of our fathers speaking louder

see see O man who is my husband
see the wiggle beneath my belly
what song is beating there?

      come O *mwali* of my sleep
          watch me
      I go to the goat to get his skin
          see me
      I go to the tree to get his bone
          listen me
      I sing to the village
      the god-sound trembles in her belly
      the god-sound walks a long safari
      come O *mwali* who the spirit blesses
          watch me
      I stretch goat-skin over hollow tree-bone
      I dance my fingers on the belly of goat
      aiwa aiwa

9

listen *mwali* of my life
watch me
listen

the goat-skin sings the boom-sound louder
    louder sings the goat-skin louder
the goat-skin sings the boom-sound louder
    sings the goat-skin louder louder
louder booms the goat-skin boom-sound louder
    louder louder

Asali

this honey you gave me
has turned to tears

dripping from your fingers
a lost sweetness

this asali you gave me
weeps its lost reasons

i am son of asali
sweet son of sweet
in the pollen air
in the floweringyears

(the taste of sugar-milk
in the memory of a once-child)

i am son of asali
who sees you in the garden
roofed with glass

10

whose flowers attract no bees

i am son of asali
the wind wrestles with my wishes
our wings
separated
by directions

come from your dome of
barren seasons

the sound of breaking glass
the taste of asali-honey
the wind wrestling with my wishes
your trembling hands
covering my memory

i am son of asali
o woman who the spirit
beckons

watch how i am weaving
your fingers flowing like rivers
of weeping silk.

Love Song of a Lamb

          i speak to you
o ram of strength
o ram of beauty
          why do you come
          toward me leaning
          behind my horned shadow?

why do you come
to me with a two-tongued
two-headed look
leaping from thine eyes?

i speak to you
o ram of power
o ram of grace
do you think
i do not see *nyoka**
the snake coiled
in the bush of thine eyes?
nyoka's venom of lust
is sapping thy strength
is killing thy beauty
overbearing hoof you are
rampaging goat
old conquering deceiver
snaking hook

head of the herd of ego
sham in a coat of lies
away from me away
i rather *nyuki* the wasp sting me

away from me
if you are coming to redress
thy worn hollow horn
i rather *chui* the leopard fang me
if you are coming to possess me
and not live and share with me
i rather simba roar death upon me

* Swahili words. [H. D.]

12

          i speak to you
o ram of beauty
o ram of grace
               all the suns
               all the moons of my life
               i have feared the scorn
               of that look which comes
               attacking me from the bush
               of shadows and eyes

               i wait for you
o ram of peace
o ram of love
               come to me in thy pride
               come to me in thy spirit
               come not to bribe me with
               thy strong horn and thy
               cunning look of design
               come not to me for a feast
               come to me for a festival

for remember
when Simba is bleeding thy throat
i am *mwana* the lamb who comes to thy side
enticing simba's claw of death with quicker blood
i am she of fleeing hooves
who sees when thy hoof breaks free
who sees thy head break
the crooked shadows of deceit
that weigh it down
that lean and lock thy body to the ground
i am she who sees thy horn pierce simba
and thy hoof trample the bush of *nyoka*
for remember
i am thy mate and thy strength and thy song

                    i sing to you
o ram whom i see
o ram whom i await
                    the horn of pride
                    is the victory song
                    of our enemies
                    who come to claw us and fang us
                    let us hurry to the feast
                    let us hurry to the festival
i am by thy side close by thy side
i am by thy side close by thy side
i am by thy side close and thy side

The Puppets Have a New King

Ulwaca ulooooooo!
Oh these cold white hands
manipulating
they broke us like limbs from trees
and carved Europe upon our
African masks and made puppets

Ulwalalooooo!
Bring out the Pygmy juju
Let us, like little black spears,
bore our way.

Coat of Many Fibers

Out of the red earth
and the black earth

grew the white cotton
and then came black and brown
fingers picking it.

In the kerosene-lighted
shadows of the evening shack
the fingers wove
a long cloak of cotton.

With a line of blood,
a thread of weeping and moaning,
a strain of song,
a streak of tears,
and a grasp on the white fiber,
the fingers spun a hymn to God.

Son of Msippi

Up
from Msippi I grew.
(Bare walk and cane stalk
make a hungry belly talk.)
Up
from the river of death.
(Walk bare and stalk cane
make a hungry belly talk.)

Up
from Msippi I grew.
Up
from the river of pain.

Out of the long red earth dipping, rising,
spreading out in deltas and plains,

out of the strong black earth turning
over by the iron plough,

out of the swamp green earth dripping
with moss and snakes,

out of the loins of the leveed lands
muscling its American vein:
the great Father of Waters,
I grew
up,
beside the prickly boll of white,
beside the bone-filled Mississippi
rolling on and on,
breaking over,
cutting off,
ignoring my bleeding fingers.

Bare stalk and sun walk
I hear a boll-weevil talk
cause I grew
up
beside the ox and the bow,
beside the rock church and the shack row,
beside the fox and the crow,
beside the melons and maize,
beside the hound dog,
beside the pink hog,
flea-hunting,
mud-grunting,
cat-fishing,
dog pissing
in the Mississippi
rolling on and on,

ignoring the colored coat I spun
of cotton fibers.

Cane-sweat river-boat
nigger-bone floating.

Up from Msippi
I grew,
wailing a song with every strain.

Woman gone woe man too
baby cry rent-pause daddy flew.

Black Star Line

My black mothers I hear them singing.

      Sons, my sons,
dip into this river with your ebony cups
A vessel of knowledge sails under power.
Study stars as well as currents.
Dip into this river with your ebony cups.

My black fathers I hear them chanting.

      Sons, my sons,
let ebony strike the blow that launches the ship!
Send cargoes and warriors back to sea.
Remember the pirates and their chains of nails.
Let ebony strike the blow that launches this ship.
Make your heads not idle sails, blown about
by any icy wind like a torn page from a book.
      Bones of my bones,

17

all you golden-black children of the sun,
lift up! and read the sky
written in the tongue of your ancestors.
It is yours, claim it.
Make no idle sails, my sons,
make heavy-boned ships that break a wave and pass it.
Bring back sagas from Songhay, Kongo, Kaaba,
deeds and words of Malik, Toussaint, Marcus,
statues of Mahdi and a lance of lightning.
Make no idle ships.
Remember the pirates.
For it is the sea who owns the pirates,
not the pirates the sea.

My black mothers I hear them singing.

      Children of my flesh,
dip into this river with your ebony cups.
A ship of knowledge sails unto wisdom.
Study what mars and what lifts up.
Dip into this river with your ebony cups.

from Jackhammer

I

The jackjack backing back and stacking stone
city-stone into cracked hydraulic echoes of dust
this jackjack hammering down the industrial crust
this jackjack is a man
I see the long historical chord pumping the man
this jackjack in the city groin
pumping the man

down
the man I see is a man long back before the jack
hammering down himself in the black sweat
under the steam locomotion
stammering under the weight of his blow
the man I see
long before the jackjack on the concrete
long before the blackman spent himself
in the womb of time hiding in the earth
long before the blackman struck

Root Song

Once when I was tree
flesh came and worshiped at my roots.
My ancestors slept in my outstretched
limbs and listened to flesh
praying and entreating on his knees.

Once when I was free
African sun woke me up green at dawn.
African wind combed the branches of my hair.
African rain washed my limbs.
African soil nourished my spirit.
African moon watched over me at night.
Once when I was tree
flesh came to sacrifice at my foot,
flesh came to preserve my voice,
flesh came honoring my limbs
as drums, as canoes, as masks,
as cathedrals and temples of the ancestor-gods.

Now flesh comes with metal teeth,
with chopping sticks,
and firelaunchers,
and flesh cuts me down,
and enslaves my limbs to make
forts, ships, pews for other gods,
stockades, flesh pens,
and crosses hung high to sacrifice gods.

Now flesh laughs at my charred and beaten
frame, discarding me in the mud, burning
me up in flames.
Now flesh listens no more to the voice
of the spirits talking through my limbs.

Flesh has grown dull at the ears now.
Flesh has grown pale and lazy.
Flesh has sinned against the fathers.
If flesh would listen I would warn him
that the spirits are displeased
and are planning what to do with him.
But flesh thinks I am dead, charred and gone.

Flesh thinks that by fire he can kill,
thinks that with metal teeth, I die,
thinks that chaining me in alien temples
with new gods carved upon my skin,
thinks that all the voices
linked from root to limb are silenced,
thinks that by cutting me down,
I will sing and dance no more,
but flesh is lazy and clogged with fat.

Flesh does not know that he
did not give me life,
nor can he take it away.

That is what the spirits are singing now.
It is time that flesh
bow down on his knee again!

Fire Bird

The fire bird has come again
Trees blow red
where once green
paddled the summer wing.

The great oak,
hugging my window,
sheds and shakes
with shivering fingers.

Every year the fire bird comes.
It is not his beauty
that I meditate,
Rather his awesome message!

"I burn them up now.
Someday I will get you."

The Temple at Ilhadan

The temple at Ilhadan is filled today.
A solemn white cloud shrouds the village.
Yesterday, I would not have gone to the temple.
But today . . . today the temple is filled.

There is no shouting in Ilhadan today.
The people are bowing in the temple.

And the long-eared cattle will not eat hill-grass
until the temple is empty.
The dogs will not bark at the sheep
until the temple is empty.
The streets of colored sea-rock will not shine
until the temple is empty.
The children who sing to the fishermen
will not sing
until the temple is empty.
The old priest who stutters and nods at the gate
will not stutter and nod
until the temple is empty.
The young girls who wear bright red
and the young men who chase them
will not laugh and fling their arms
until the temple is empty.
For the sun will not shine again in Ilhadan
until death himself has passed away.

I am going to the temple.
The dust of the road wraps around my legs,
and behind the grey sky of Ilhadan
the sun drowns itself in tears.
Death came a year ago and left the temple full.
Today he has come again.
Yesterday we celebrated a victory in Ilhadan,
but today we are not sure if we won at all.
There is no shouting of songs,
only weeping and bowing in the temple.

Yesterday we sang of today, but today is here.
The songs are forgotten and buried as dreams.

Now we know about tomorrow:
Tomorrow is only the waiting for tomorrow.
The victories of yesterday grow dimmer
like the fading of the color in the evening sky.

I shall not stay long in the temple.
I will hurry away and reach the Pool of Sheemz
before the crowds and there I will
bathe the dust from my feet
and watch the evening gather in the west.

And tomorrow I will not come to the temple.
Tomorrow the long-eared cattle will be hungry.
The old priest will give blessings at the gate
and fall asleep beside the pool.
And after the rain, the sun will shine upon
the streets of colored sea-rock,
there will be shouting and singing,
and the temple at Ilhadan will be empty.

Somnus

Sleep is like death, as mysterious as the sea, but unlike death,
it is like the dream of the lotus, and in that way, one can ask
what is the meaning of the mirage of the lotus?

I
A mask and a measure he wears
of the lotus
I have taken of the lotus
wake me wake me
A flash of lotus oil he bears

II

In my dreams I sleep
And the Styx bears me up
My bones, ship wrecked,
sink.

of the lotus
I am shaken by the lotus
break me break me
A mirage is the mask he wears

III

Thru the window of dream
I see the wide seas
shimmering like fire
on horizons
He sits, indifferent pirate,
counting all eyes that see beyond
his mask.

of the lotus
I am anointed by the lotus
of the lotus
wake me wake me!
before we sleep
before we dream

Somnus (*Alternate version*)

I

Wild reeds hugged by the wind
speak of legs and skyscrapers,
of music, Archimedes and sin.

24

of the lotus
I have eaten of the lotus
of the lotus
when must I wake you?

Wet faces wrestling with the sea
blow memories of their genesis
that transfix and electrocute me.
> *of the lotus*
> *I have eaten of the lotus*
> *of the lotus*
> *when must I shake you?*

Perhaps, I have never eaten whale,
nor has a whale ever swallowed me.
Perhaps I have never been in any kind of jail.
> *but of the lotus*
> *I have eaten of the lotus*
> *of the lotus*
> *when must I break you?*

The sea and the sky bear witness to the truth:
my memory and my message
ask questions of youth.
> *of the lotus*
> *I have eaten of the lotus*
> *of the lotus*
> *when must I take you?*

II
I have made demi-gods of the ages
where drunken lovers
fall heirs to myths and sages.
Philosophy and science:

two sails billowed by the wind,
two faces like ours,
wrestling with the sea.

Locked in my oceanic prism
I am the embryo that covers you
and releases us from sleep's prison.
Wild reeds hugged by the wind
bow and rise.
Let us reckon with the sea and the lotus:
demi-gods circling above and below us.

Of the lotus
I have taken of the lotus
the sea and the sky bear witness to the truth
wet faces wrestling with the sea
of the lotus
I am broken by the lotus
of the lotus
of the lotus, careful of the lotus

Island Within Island

our voices waved upwards into a tide
that wrapped itself around the island
like some great blue snake and i
with visions unravelled my body
from the great octopus i had slain
with our voices

across the island i carried my
soul as one would carry a tiny
baby found starving and dying

back leaving skin shedding
and merging with the tentacles
of the rotting world
my voice walks like a skeleton

i have reached the edge of lagoon
protected in the curve of the tidal
rhythms are beating down my bones
the island has appeared
floating perhaps beckoning me
to its water free of beasts
our voices are saying to our voices

i am the center and the sense
i am the sun
out of me comes everything

A Natural Man

Ikef

When I was three
I blew icons of milk
from sweet pipes of flesh
and giggled at the eye-bubbles
giving me pleasure.

When I was six
I blew icons of soap
from wooden pipes
and chased little girls
on giant bubble-dragons.

When I was nine
I blew hero rings
from stolen cigarettes
and staggered over
smoke-ropes of lies.

When I was twelve
I blew kisses on paper
to big girls
who broke my bubbles
with knowing eyes.

When I was fifteen
I blew icons of pleasure

from a horn, dreaming
of milk, crystal spheres,
and warriors eating honey.

When I was eighteen
I smoked icons of kef
and blew images
that spun and exploded,
reflecting visions of three.

Knees of a Natural Man

(for Jay Wright)

my ole man took me to the fulton fish market
we walk around in the guts and the scales

my ole man show me a dead fish, eyes like throat spit
he say "you hongry boy?" i say "naw, not yet"

my ole man show me how to pick the leavings
he say people throw away fish that not rotten

we scaling on our knees back uptown on lenox
sold five fish, keepin one for the pot

my ole man copped a bottle of wine
he say, "boy, build me a fire out in the lot"

backyard cat climbin up my leg for fish
i make a fire in the ash can

my ole man come when he smell fish
frank williams is with him, they got wine

32

my ole man say "the boy cotch the big one"
he tell big lie and slap me on the head

i give the guts to the cat and take me some wine
we walk around the sparks like we in hell

my ole man is laughin and coughin up wine
he say "you hongry boy?" i say "naw, not yet"

next time i go to fulton fish market
first thing i do is take a long drink of wine

Harlem Gulp

I
like ailing crabs
jay-scuttling
circles over sooted stone beach

like squawking blackbirds
pecking
mites in the circle of sun

we tremble off snow

like black pearls
trapped
in the white cerebellum
we glisten out of reach

of drum-gun and talking bird

we give our children
broken feathers
praying the jesus disease
that they lance the tumor
before it is time to fly

II
like skeletons
trekking behind Olorun
we wait for flesh and sight
we stand in our jail-like
shadows
if we can believe in skeletons
we know we shall fly
before we die before the light

My Little Boy

My little boy speaks
with an accent.
I must remember sometime
to lean my head down
and whisper in his ear
and ask him the name
of the country
he comes from.
I like his accent.

The Playground Is My Home

"you kids git out from there 'fore
somebody throw somethin on your heads!"

that's the lady on the fifth floor
i see her yesterday she throw somethin out
we kids playing in the backyard
we move into the alley.
a lot of garbage in the alley
we climb over the bed mattress and
i grab me a fist full of cotton
and throw it up in the sky

"rainin cotton, rainin cotton."

Sanctuary

(to Ralph and Jeanne Cebulla)

If I were an eye
peering through
the telescopic sun column
that magnifies this ice forest,
I would see that cardinal
like a burning phoenix . . .

The icicle prism
explodes!

Is this mosaic the brush strokes
of some random master
residing in the circles
of my eyes?

The Cardinal

I do not believe that red on the scientific table
can be so fed and winglessly able
to break the hunger of beasts
flying outside my jail cell
like comic clowns

nor blood measured and typed
could design or define
funerals or feasts
that is old
the cardinal has no red name like fire or crown

Rose Jungle

(to Hale Chatfield)

For thirty-one years he planted roses,
until the withered structure of the house
became thorned flesh.
At night he would lie
exhausted and crucified.

For thirty-one years he had planted.
From the road I could see only
a mountain of roses growing wild.

"Why don't you train the stems
to bow?" I asked.

"The wind is the better teacher," he said.

"Why don't you trim their arms?"

"In due time these arms will
embrace the earth.
I will not lessen their love."

Mexico Through a Clear Window

I want you to sit perfectly still
    until the boat reaches that tongue
    of spray which will baptize us.

Then I want you to leap high in the sky
    with me until we see
    yellow trees and the blue gulf.

Ghosts

Always I wait for the trees to fall
down begging,
their outstretched prayers
prostrate across my path,
and then I am sure that I am sleep.

Last nite we made two shadows disrobe,
and we sat beside the fire
where the moon had watched over us
the nites before,
and we—you and I—fleshed each other.

I am sick of these weeping half-days
that come out of the past—
feathers lost in a wind berserk—

and clog the mind with ideas of morning.
Flesh remembers when it *is*.

Always the shadows disrobe us with eyes—
let the moon dream itself a sun—
and we dance as we dance now . . .
Always I recall this drowsiness falling
upon me as I take my place.

A Song of Flesh

Wild stallions raced across the barren stretches
of my brain.
Eagles broke the tornado currents of my breath
with fire wings and razor talons.
A tiger fish slashed the shores of my blood.
When I awoke,
I took the sleeping mountains of your breasts
tenderly tenderly
between my quivering lips
and I guillotined the stallions,
drowned the eagles,
and drove the tiger fish back
into the sea of your heart.

Full Moon

The circle moon
fell upon your face.
The circle moon
spilled powdered shadows

upon your shape.
The moon, the circle moon
argued with me,
fell upon my arms
and told me that I could
gather up all the dust of
the circle night
and I could tell you
woman
I love you.

If I Were Earth

Each tear that fell
from the crushed
moons of your face,
stabbed me,
broke and split
into a thousand pains.
But I held out my arms,
and not one did I miss,
no, not one pain.
And if I don't let
you soak into me
and bring me up,
if I don't let you seep
deep into me
and teach me,
then you can cry in
the morning to the sun,
and tell him to rise up
and burn me away.

Love Song

Beloved,
I have to adore the earth:

The wind must have heard
your voice once.
It echoes and sings like you.

The soil must have tasted
you once.
It is laden with your scent.

The trees honor you
in gold
and blush when you pass.

I know why the north country
is frozen.
It has been trying to preserve
your memory.

I know why the desert
burns with fever.
It has wept too long without you.

On hands and knees,
the ocean begs up the beach,
and falls at your feet.

I have to adore
the mirror of the earth.
You have taught her well
how to be beautiful.

Valentines

Forgive me if I have not sent you
a valentine
but I thought you knew
that you already have my heart
Here take the space where my
heart goes
I give that to you too

Where the
Sidewalk Ends

Afro-American

my black mother birthed me
    my white mother girthed me
my black mother suckled me
    my white mother sucked me in
my black mother sang to me
    my white mother sanctified me
    she crucified me

my black mother is a fine beautiful thang
she bathed me and died for me
she stitched me together, took me into her
bosom and mixed her tears with mine
little black baby i was wretched
a shadow without a body, fatherless, sunless
my black mother shook sweet songs and sweat
all over me and her sugar and her salt saved me

    my white mother is a whore
    with the holy white plague
    a hollow cross between Martha and Mary
    she looked at me and screamed bastard!
    she left me light of body and of mind
    she took what my black mother gave me
    and left me half blind

bone is my black mother
ivory stone
strength is my black mother
my ancient skeletal home
force is my black mother
she maintains and transforms

my black mother is a long-haired sensuous river
where the Kongo flows into the Mississippi she
is coming where my father's blood rises in jets
and like rain, glows, transformed red, tan, black
I am growing in the bosom and in the loins
of America
born and knitted in the soil, when I finish growing
you can pick me up as you would a rare and fabulous
seed and you can
blow Africa
on me as you would a holy reed.

If You Behave

Well now,
I'll saint you but I wont haint you
I'll test you but I wont touch you
I'll fake you but I wont brake you
you know what I mean?
I'll hook you but I wont spook you
thas all IF YOU BEHAVE!

Well now,
I could rock you but I wouldnt sock you
I might feint you but I wouldnt taint you

46

I could rap to you but I wouldnt slap you
you dig what I mean?
I'll walk you but I wouldnt stalk you
thas all IF YOU BEHAVE!

Well now,
I'll plead you but I wouldn't bleed you
I might put the word on you but not the sword on you
I could butt you but I wouldnt cut you
you understand?
I'll smack you but I wont attack you
thas of course IF YOU BEHAVE!

Well now,
there one little bit I got to say
(you can get off your knees
you dont have to pray)
thas all if you behave yourself
YOU DAMN SURE WILL SAVE YOURSELF

Knock on Wood

i go out to totem street
        we play
        neon monster
                and watusi feet

killer sharks chasin behind
        we play hide
        siren!
                and out-run cops
they catch
        willie

and me
        splittin over fence
they knock
        in willie's head
        hole
they kick me watusi
        down
                for dead
like yesterday
        runnin feet in my brain
        won't stop willie lookin blood
                beggin me
cut off blackjack pain

so whenever you see me comin
        crazy watusi
                you call me watusi
i keep a wooden willie
        blade and bone outa that fence
a high willie da conqueror
        listen! up there he talkin
wooden willie got all the sense

i go out to siren street
        don't play no more
me and willie beat a certain beat
        aimin wood carvin shadows

sometimes i knock on wood
        with fist
me and willie play *togetherin*
        and we don't miss

I Laugh Talk Joke

i laugh talk joke
smoke dope skip rope, may take a coke
jump up and down, walk around
drink mash and talk trash
beat a blind baby over the head
with a brick
knock a no-legged man to his
bended knees
cause i'm a movin fool
never been to school
god raised me and the devil
praised me
catch a preacher in a boat
and slit his throat
pass a church,
I might pray
but don't fuck with me
cause i don't play

Ascension

the black kite
wooden bones cracking against the wind
escaped from black fingers
with a holy shout
Jesus, ascending, yet
hung from the black umbilical string

there are eagles in the skies
the paper soul is my last prayer
when i am a child i play
the black kite in my sight

hangs
when i am a man i put away toys
Jesus pulling me up and up
yet my feet on the ground

there are eagles who see this game
the paper soul is my last

when the kite
(hung in heaven)
falls
i am sure my string has run out
the game is over

i will never find the holy vapor
falling yonder

the black kite is white
spun from black fingers
(children learning to write)

i will turn my back
where bones tumble
the game is over

i see the eagle
and the eagle sees me

beyond that . . . ?

Black Trumpeter

we must kill our gods before they kill us
not because we will to kill but because

our gods think themselves gods
they are always actors who have lost their script
cannot remember the lines, and fake visions
of themselves without mirrors
phantoms screaming without voices

we must kill our gods before they kill us
this then is the law and the testament
with malice toward none we give you warning
when the statute falls the pedestal remains
black birds do not light upon the roots of trees
the wing praises the root by taking to the limbs
we are Americans looking in the mirror of Africa

The Zebra Goes Wild Where the Sidewalk Ends

I
Neon stripes tighten my wall
where my crayon landlord hangs
from a bent nail.

My black father sits crooked
in the kitchen
drunk on Jesus' blood turned
to cheap wine.

In his tremor he curses
the landlord who grins
from inside the rent book.

My father's eyes are
bolls of cotton.

He sits upon the landlord's
operating table.
the needle of the nation
sucking his soul.

II
Chains of light race over
my stricken city.
Glittering web spun by
the white widow spider.

I see this wild arena
where we are harnessed
by alien electric shadows.

Even when the sun washes
the debris
I will recall my landlord
hanging in my room
and my father moaning in
Jesus' tomb.

In America all zebras
are in the zoo.

I hear the piston bark
and ibm spark:
let us program rabies.
the madness is foaming now.

No wild zebras roam the American plain.
The mad dogs are running.
The African zebra is gone into the dust.

I see the shadow thieves coming
and my father on the specimen table.

Decision, Says the Source

Decision, says the Source
links precision.
Choose the one to strike
and strike hard.
The nail becomes
Desire.
The anvil rings fire.
Decision, says the Source
cleans the inner chambers
of the mind.
Light enters and reveals
confusion.
Decision, says the Source
has two wings of light
one fusion the other precision.

Montage

... the street walked in front
of me and by lamp eyes the people
grew up like stone thoughts
cemented to the height of the
steel sky where twice a dog
barked once from that window
and somebody was watching me
hiding behind that curtain face

near the wall and I do not know
if the curtain was painted
male or female or a barking
sky beneath the tall street
walking into thoughts of brick
and bone behind me where I was ...

Lash—American Yankee Song

lash
I take it from you for nothing

lash
the lynched tree mocks you for me
ropes your shadow to the ground
and defies your black heart to cry a sound

lash
I love to hate the difference of you
beaten under the beating tree lost
beneath seas drowning in the negative

lash
I take it from you for nothing
the conqueror I am staking my ships
with your stacked bones breaking
under my boot growing bigger and bigger

lash
I rake it out for nothing because I
am sent of God to kill the burnt remnants
of his mistakes because I am the top
half of the sphere of his head

lash
I take it away from you for nothing
learning you and hating my learning
because it is you that I learn and
you who knows the tree better than me

lash
I subtract it from you because I need
because I must add to my creed that
which is the seed of the tree and since
I am God and do not know then who?

lash
for you this is meant lash
upon the nigger bent lash
down upon the holy word lash
upon the God who is unheard

lash
I am sorry lash to have to borrow
lash your soul lash to carry
mine lash the day and the night
lash I am the taker of the booty lash you lash

Tis of Thee

1.
You are oversized, you are overrated, you are overblown,
fat and filled with hardened rocks.
You are sick and stumbling like an old man without
a stick in the mud.
You make me sick to my stomach, and I am sad
that I have to look at you.

You have eaten too much garlic
and drunk too much beer,
and built too many empty churches.
You are fat with starch and lies.

2.

Your steeled cities range like malignant cancers across
the belly of your land.
Your sons race death in metal machines that
defecate poison into the air.
Your ideas are machine made,
your values operated by machines
your truths nourished by machines,
your history written by machines,
your language sounds like millions of coins jingling
into an empty barrel.
Your heroes are dead.
Your wars are massacres.
You are an overkiller,
oversexed, overripe, overrotten.

3.

You are a sinful old man who has no repentance
in his heart,
a lecherous old winebelly vomiting blood.
You are a murderer of your sons
and a raper of your daughters.
You are cold and filled with death.
Few flowers grow from your gardens
and the snow and the ice shall be your grave.

4.

You are a despiser of black and misunderstander of white.
You are a mystery of yourself and a hater of that.
You once were a star that blazed,

but now you are overcivilized, oversterilized, oversated.
If you were a barren tree in my garden
I would come and cut you down.

Mosaic Harlem

what news from the bottle?
      rats shedding hair in ice
      nodding veins filled with snow
      blackeyed peas, grits, red rice
through the broken glass I hear a breaking age
what song do we gurgle?

what news from the bottom?
      Jesus learning judo
      I scratch giant lice and ghetto
      fleas in the gutter of my mind
the sucking boll weevil converts to blood
when will the mosquito fear the rage under sweat?

what view from the bottle?
      cats pawing at cotton ideas
      the roach in the milk
      crawls safely to the nipple
why is green not black, brown, tan, only pain?
this hombre is a tiger rose star of sneaky david.

what news from the bureau?
      a mole stoking coal in wine-steam and no gas
      building baby foundations from lamb-bone
      pray in Chinese, farting in English
I hear a black drum roaring up a green lion on yellow silk
come to kill the keeper of our cage

what news from James' bastard bible?
    al-Mahdi kneels in the mosque,
    Melchizedek, Moses, Marcus, Muhammad, Malcolm!
    marshalling words, mobilizing swords
the message is mixed and masticated with Martin
the god news of the gospel is crossing a crescent

what they do at the bottom?
    went to the cop and he took my pot
    the law giveth and the law taketh away
    I can neither pee nor blow
they will rope Mary and take pussy for my bail
I will remember, I will recall, bottoms up, I cop

what news from the black bastille?
    ram of god busting up shit
    unicorning the wolf, panthering the fox
    the old shepherd is himself lost
the ram will not stop, what news from the bottom?
the east! the west! and the top!

Blues Songs

Low Down Dog Blues

Went to my baby's back door, my baby say she aint home
Yeah my baby holler she just aint home
But if you aint got no meat baby,
                    please throw your dog a bone

Standin in her back yard, my long tail tucked under
Standin in the back yard, my long tail tucked way under
Cryin so many tears, my baby think it's lightnin and thunder

Got them low down dog blues, people, my sniffer can't find
            no bait
It's the low down dog blues, when your sniffer can't find
            no bait
Just whinin for my baby to please open up her gate

Well, she aint heard my barkin, this dog better hit the trail
Yeah, guess a low down dog better hit the trail
That woman dont even care when a good dog wag his tail

Keep the Faith Blues

They say if you ain't got no faith
                    you keep the blues most all the time
If you ain't got no faith, you keep the blues most all the time
Must be the reason I'm almost bout to lose my mind

I'm tryin to hold on, people, tryin to keep what I got
Yeah, tryin to hold on, tryin hard to keep what I got
But you know the man is steadyin pressin me
                    bout to bust my natural back

Heard a man say once, you better hold on and keep the faith
He said hold on baby, and keep the faith
People, I swear I'm hold on and all I got *left* is faith

Yes the world gone crazy, they even talk about God is dead
Yes the world is gone crazy, some say worship the Devil
          instead

Well, I'm keepin my own faith, people
Can't let religion
                    bust open my head.

Machines Can Do It Too
(IBM Blues)

Looky hear folks, you all better watch out
I say looky hear y'all, better watch out
They got machines pickin cotton and machines cure the gout

Yeah! They got machines that walk and talk
                    even sing a song to you

They got machines fly and cry,
                    even wave bye bye to you
They got'em to make you happy
                got'em to make you blue

My baby wouldnt let me in last night
                just wouldnt answer my ring
My baby wouldnt let me in last night
                just wouldnt answer my ring
I got to leave this old country
                when they machines doin everything

Let me tell you people, tell you what I have to do
Let me tell it like it is people,
                tell you what I have to do
If I find a machine in bed with me,
                that's the time I'm through

Standin Tall Blues

Now you say my shoes runover and my hair's long and nappy
Yeah my shoes runover, my hair long and nappy
But you know where your bread and meat comin from baby
                it sure make you happy

Now we walkin down town baby, fightin the mean ole hawk
All bundled up, fightin that mean ole hawk
You lookin in the window, say you need a mink coat

Now that's alright baby, I work hard and my head is nappy
Yeah my shoes runover and my head is nappy
But when you need heat for your cooker
                you come runnin to pappy

So dont worry bout how I look baby
                         that aint it at all
Dont worry bout looks pretty baby
                         that aint it at all
You cant hide it cause I ride it
                         that's me standin tall

Pills and Chills Blues

Baby, I told you oncet bout takin them pills
Yeah I done told you bout takin them pills
You stay in the bed talkin bout you got the chills

What they tryin to do? slow down my population?
What they tryin to do? cut off my population?
Dont they know I got a long civilization?

Now all you women, listen to a bit of Hank's advice
I say I got just a little piece of advice
Make your man put a ring on your finger
                    Then you treat his population nice

Baby when the doctor pass you them pills,
                    hold out you finger, show'im your new ring
Just hold out your hand woman, show'im your ring
And dont forget to tell him,
                    that we got that rhythm thing!

Employment Blues

I been to the factory, even got a card to go to sea
Yeah, I even got a card to merchant the sea
Aint there somebody in this city got a job for poor me?

Been all over town, everybody say the same
Yes, they all sayin the same
I'm so desperated, think I'll change my name

Gettin interviewed the other day, man say, "Sit down boy"
Yeah, outa work and he say "Sit down boy"
Well I looked at the man and I say, "My fist look like a toy?"

Lookin high and low people
                              drive a truck or dig a ditch
Yeah, I'll drive a truck or dig a ditch

Cause without a job, a man's in an awful fix

Early Bird Blues

They tell me the early bird catches the worm
Yeah, the early bird catches the worm
You comin in mighty late baby
                    got a feelin somethin's wrong

I'm gonna investigate the state of things baby
                    check your scene in and out
Got to investigate you baby
                    check your scene in and out
I'm gonna FBI you baby,
                    might have to lock up my house

Dont mind you goin out baby
                like you say "to see a show"
Now, I dont mind baby
                if you see your show
But they dont sell whisky in movies
                and I dont like whispers at my door

Yes, I got my trigger cocked baby
                got aim on a movin head
Yeah, got my trigger cocked
                watchin for a movin head
When I catch him baby, you better duck
                or you be dead

Outer Space Blues

(to Sun Ra Myth)

People, I heard the news the other day
                like to scared me half to death
Yeah things happen in this world
                like to scared me half to death
TV say a spaceship is comin here
                if it do wont be no people left

But I tell you folks, spaceship cant be so bad
Reckon I just a fool people,
                spaceship cant be too bad
I been on earth all my life,
                and all my life I been mad

So when the spaceship land
                I aint runnin too fast
I say, I reckon I might not run too fast

I might run over into Mississippi
        and you know I can't pass

Hold it people, I see a flying saucer comin
        guess I wait and see
Yeah, a spaceship comin
        guess I wait and see
All I know they might look just like me

Uncle Sam Uptight Blues

Well, baby if the man's uptight
        you know how I am
Well, if Uncle Sam is uptight baby
        you know how I am
He puttin copper in his silver
        uptight done got to Uncle Sam

Well, he puttin more pep in his gas
        but his cars wont start
  (*repeat*)
Got safety gadgets in the new ones
        half of 'em fallin apart

Uncle Sam is uptight baby
        not a friend in sight
World wont listen to him baby
        not a friend in sight
Maybe Mr Uptight is my buddy
        come to make Uncle do right

Now the man know I aint scared of him
        so he keeps a foot on my back

Yeah, Uncle stays on my back
He know the Chinaman aint yellow
      He heard somebody say the chinaman might be black

The Buster

Now when I was a kid, my mama
                use to bust me with a switch
      (I was bad)   [*Spoken*]
Now my mama used to bust me with a switch
Now my baby scream "Bust me" and I buster,
                cause she so sweet

Now this a dance the buster you gotta learn
Do the buster, a dance you gotta learn
It'll make you wanto shout,
              make your buster burn

Now you put your right foot here
              your left foot there
Do a little bustin here a little bustin there
Now what you do with your hands,
             I'm tellin you I dont care

Do the buster one, baby it's good, buster two
Hmmmm buster one, hmmmm buster two

Dance the buster the whole night through

Mailman Blues

Mailman, mailman what's takin you so long?
Hurry mailman, what's takin you so long?
With my baby's letter takin your time is wrong

Now yesterday no letter
                but you brought my welfare check
Today aint no better
                done spent my welfare check
If I dont hear from my baby,
                I swear I'll be a wreck

Well they say he gone and left me
                left me holdin the bag
My baby done left me
                left me holdin the bag
Now you cant buy butter on welfare
                and being broke with margarine is a drag

Mailman when you come dig deep in your sack
Please mailman dig up a letter from your sack
I think my baby done left me and I got to get on his track

Grandma's Got a Wig

Now I peeped in the closet
                I know why grandma's lookin so good
Yeah, think I know why's grandma's lookin so good
Grandma's got a red wig, baby
                she's swingin like I know she could

Yeah, Granny's got her wig on now
                Grandpa's give her the eye

Yeah, Granny's got her wig on
                    Grandpa's give her the koochy eye
Well, I think I'm gonna buy you a wig baby,
                    so I won't have to say bye-bye

Yeah, Granny's got her wig on now
                    and granpa's got his shirt half off
Yeah, a pretty red wig,
                    granpa's got his shirt half off
Well, I dont mind you wearin a wig baby
                    but dont cut your nappy hair off

Yeah, Granny's got her wig on now
                    and granpa's workin on his shoes
Yeah, a pretty red wig
                    granpa's takin off his shoes
Keep you wig on pretty baby,
                    or I have to sing the nappy haired blues

Concentration Camp Blues

I aint jokin people, I aint playin around
Wouldnt jive you people, aint playin around
They got the Indian on the reservation
                    got us in the ghetto town

Like when you down home, tryin to get out
A mule in his stall trying to kick out
You gets to it in the ghetto but you aint got out

Wouldn't jive you people, this a natural fact
They watchin us all people, a natural fact
The man is plannin to put a harness on my back

So get with it people, let's get outa his camp
I aint jokin, I got to get outa his camp
Cause the man is ready to number us all with a rubber stamp

Out of Work Blues

Well I went down to the state office
                        lookin for a job
Yeah went down to the man
                        got to have some kinda job
Fell in the place and the place was a mob

Now I dont mind work, do it all the time
Dont mind a little work when I can find the time
But I dont like standin all day on the wrong line

And you know one thing, my feet subject to quit
Yeah standin too long, my feet subject to quit
And when that happen, y'all know I got to sit

Now you 'magine how I feel when the man say
                        he closin
Waitin all day long and the man say
                        he closin
Hurt me people, specially when I was sittin in the corner
                        one eye winkin one eye dozin

Too Hot to Handle Blues

You cant touch me baby, I'm too hot for the hand
Hear me? Dont touch me baby, you burn your hand
But I stay with you tonight and you can keep me if you can

I keep you warm baby, I'm a burning coal
O its good baby

Listen to the Sound of My Horn!

Music and I . . . have come at last!

Mississippi Song

I was a mist in the caverns
of your mind.
I was without shape, without sound,
without color, without depth,
without voice,
and then I heard distant voices
moaning in the night,
and I felt my people calling me.

Heated, I expanded.
I broke your skull-bone.

And I found your face looking
at me: dark lines waiting for the light.

Come, my people,
we have work to do.
All the days of my capture I dreamed
of seeing you.
Come, we will put the bones together.
We will stand in the sun and make a sound
with uplifted voices.
We will let the sun splatter a thousand
colors over our skins.
We will reach down into our souls and bring
up the son of man.
We will call the world by our name.
We will give the world our voice.
We will sing.
And when we sing, they will hear us,
and they will remember the days
of calling out, the days of groaning,
and they will sing with us,
and then I will say:

I was mist.
Now I am water.

Pane of Vision

They stand upon their shadows near the
    crooked line in the sands
and they strain to see the day's birth
    against the sky which sucks
their sight and every force upon the land.

In the blindness of the morning,
    in the lightning pain of seeing,
they are born, and in a flash, die.

Between the eternal moments
    the world is their slave
and their destroyer.

They are not born to their society.
    Like wanderers
they walk the shores of time
    searching for a light before
their eyes.

And the pain, the pain, the pain
    of knowing that the pain is
eternal, that the sky shall lift up
    and rain them down
and blind their eyes.

They are not born to their world.
It is born to them.
An eternal union.
As the day is born
the night dies.
Upon the edge of the pane
they stand.

It is only when they sing
and the great pane shatters
and the thunder stabs
and the earth shudders,

it is only then
that they sing their song
and their society listens and awakes. . . .

Come, it is time to be born.

i saw the sky

i saw the sky red above the tree-line
of the far hills and i remembered how you
tasted . . .
like fire
i saw the sky red below the blue-black
and i wanted to write you letters
and books and poems and dictionaries
not as a gift to win you
not to pay for you
but to illuminate the greater part
of ourselves
to add structure to the music we hear
to add dimension to sound
to prove that one plus one equals two

Green Hill Golden Mountain

Do you remember the honeysuckle hill in the dawn?
   You were passing down,
    but I sang to you
   and you lifted your head.

Do you remember the sweet pain of turning around?
   I was at the crest
   and I saw hope stretching
   golden arms from the horizon
   where a glittering mountain
   leaped into the skies.

Do you remember the country we saw there?
　　The snags and the thorns
　　were clutching at your gown
　　and the hill of earth
　　was leading you down,
　　but then the dawn broke
　　above the hill and I waved
　　honeysuckles at you. . . .

Do you remember the sweet pain of turning around?
　　The light bathed the green hill
　　and it danced before our eyes,
　　remember? I beckoned
　　and almost . . .
　　you came. . . .

Do you remember that honeysuckle hill in the dawn?
　　The height of joy.
　　But the only thing
　　we could do, remember?
　　was look with our eyes.
　　And then remember how,
　　on separate paths,
we climbed the mountain in the skies?

Listen To the Sound of My Horn

Listen to the sound of my horn . . .
　　this note you have longed to hear.
Listen to the sound of my horn, I say,
　　this music you have hummed by ear.

I sound the time to rise for the fields.
I moan the rhythm as the congregation kneels.
　　I am the note of air,
　　the voice of your despair.
I cry long nights for you, my people.
I rise early, pull on my coat of cotton

and my shirt of tears
and a smile to mask my fears.
I tote water to sun-baked trembling lips,
and I sing away the pain
oozing from hips lashed by the chain of years.

But now, my people, I have a new song.
Listen America, listen every songless ear:
Now the congregation rises,
Now a burdened land sings.
Now the air breathes fresh.
Now the rain fills the buckets.
The note makes song.
The pain washes away.
And my horn of clay airs a long signal motif.

Listen to the sound of my horn, my people,
this rhythm of years long past.
Listen to the sound of my horn, I say,
Great music and I . . . have come at last!

Ode to Zambia*

Hail Zambia!
Thou art a child born of much struggle.

Hail Zambia!
Thou art another star in the sky.

Hail Zambia!
Thou art a new green sprout springing
out of Africa.

---

* Author's note: "Ode to Zambia" was dedicated to Siame B. Siamo on Independence Day of
the Republic of Zambia. It was read to an audience at Rutgers University [October 24, 1964]
and dedicated to all lovers of Freedom all over the earth.

Hail Zambia!
Thou art another voice cryin *Uhurru*!

Hail Zambia!
Zambesi will flow by you on currents of song.

Hail Zambia!
A great canoe for many warriors.

Hail Zambia!
Zimbabwe will spring up and speak to you.

Hail Zambia!
The black root will make the land green.

Hail Zambia!
And the orange eagle will rest his talons.

Hail Zambia!
Thou art a Republic, an example for us.

Your distant Brothers on the Mississippi
Salute you in Peace and Prosperity.

Sweet Wine of Rose

I press a rose into my face
        and I can even taste
        the mysterious fragrance pouring out,
        the fragrance aged by the Hand
        that squeezes my pulse.

If I could live
        and die amongst the roses!
        for sometimes my pulse throbs weak
        and I wonder if my veins
        channel some impure stinking mixture.

I crush a rose into my face:
            Ah! Sweet wine of life
            flowing through a rose,
            permeate my flesh,
            flush my veins.

Again, I urge a rose into my face:
            sacred mystery,
            intoxicating dew,
            every drop of blood inside me
            quivers. . . .

If I could drink the rose-wine,
            drink it from the Palms
            that quicken me. . . .
            if I could *live*,
            if I could *be* the red wine.

Ah, great joy . . .
            I think
                    those Hands
                            are shaping me. . . .

Take This River!

We move up a spine of earth
That bridges the river and the canal.
And where a dying white log, finger-like,
Floating off the bank, claws at the slope,
We stumble, and we laugh.
We slow beneath the moon's eye;
Near the shine of the river's blood face,
The canal's veil of underbrush sweats frost,
And this ancient watery scar retains
The motionless tears of men with troubled spirits.
For like the whole earth,
This land of mine is soaked. . . .

Shadows together,
We fall on the grass without a word.
We had run this far from the town.
We had taken the bony course, rocky and narrow,
He leading, I following.
Our breath streams into October
As the wind sucks our sweat and a leaf. . . .

"We have come a long long way, mahn."
He points over the river
Where it bends west, then east,
And leaves our sight.

"I guess we have," I pant. "I can hear
My angry muscles talking to my bones."
And we laugh.

The hood of night is coming.
Up the river, down the river
The sky and night kiss between the wind.

"You know," Ben says, "this is where
I brought Evelyn. . . .
Look. We sat on that log
And watched a river egret
Till it flew away with the evening.

"But mahn, she is a funny girl, Aiee!
But she looks like me Jamaica woman. . . .
But she asks me all the questions, mahn.
I'm going to miss her mahn, Aiee!

"But I will . . . Evvie. Evvie I love you,
But I do Evvie . . . Evvie. . . ," he says
And blows a kiss into the wind.
Broken shadows upon the canal
Form and blur, as leaves shudder again . . . again.

"Tell me this, Ben," I say.
"Do you love American girls?

You know, do most Jamaicans
Understand this country?"

We almost laugh. Our sweat is gone.
He whispers "Aiee" on a long low breath.

And we turn full circle to the river,
Our backs to the blind canal.

"But I'm not most Jamaicans. . . .
I'm only Ben, and tomorrow I'll be gone,
And . . . Evvie, I love you. . . .
Aiee! My woman, how can I love you?"

Blurred images upon the river
Flow together and we are there. . . .

"What did she ask you?" I say.
"Everything and nothing, maybe.
But I couldn't tell her all."
We almost laugh. "'Cause I
Don't know it all, mahn.

"Look, see over there. . . .
We walked down from there
Where the park ends
And the canal begins
Where that red shale rock
Down the slope there . . . see?
Sits itself up like a figure,
We first touch our hands . . .
And up floats this log.
Not in the river
But in the canal there
And it's slimy and old
And I kick it back . . .
And mahn, she does too.
Then she asks me:
'Bennie, if I cry
When you leave would you
Remember me more?'

Aiee! She's a natural goddess!
And she asks me:
'Bennie, when you think of Jamaica
Can you picture me there?'
And while she's saying this,
She's reaching for the river
Current like she's feeling its pulse.
She asks me:
'Bennie, America means something to you?
Maybe our meeting, our love? has
Something to do with America,
Like the river? Do you know Bennie?'
Aiee, Aiee, mahn I tell you
She might make me marry . . .
Aiee! Evvie, Jamaica . . . moon!
And how can I say anything?
I tell her:
'Africa, somewhere is Africa.
Do you understand,' I say to her,
And she look at me with the moon,
And I hear the wind and the leaves
And we do not laugh . . .
We are so close now no wind between us . . .
I say to her:
'Evvie, I do not know America
Except maybe in my tears. . . .
Maybe when I look out from Jamaica
Sometimes, at the ocean water. . . .
Maybe then I know this country. . . .
But I know that we, we Evvie. . . .
I know that this river goes and goes.
She takes me to the ocean,
The mother of water
And then I am home.'
And she tells me she knows
By the silence in her eyes.
I reach our hands again down
And bathe them in the night current
And I say: 'Take this river, Evvie. . . .'
Aiee, wind around us, Aiee my God!
Only the night knows how we kiss."

He stands up.
A raincloud sailing upon a leaf, whirs
In the momentary embrace of our memories. . . .
"Let's run," I say, "and warm these bones."
But he trots a bit, then stops,
Looking at his Jamaica sky.
"Let's run the long road west
Down the river road," I say,
"And I'll tell you of my woman . . . Aiee."
We laugh, but we stop.
And then, up the spiny ridge
We race through the trees
Like spirited fingers of frosty air.
We move toward some blurred
Mechanical light edged like an egret
And swallowed by the night.
Into this land of mine.
And the wind is cold, a prodding
Finger at our backs.
The still earth. Except for us.
And from behind that ebon cloak,
The moon observes. . . .
And we do not laugh
And we do not cry,
And where the land slopes,
We take the river. . . .
But we do not stumble,
We do not laugh,
We do not cry,
And we do not stop. . . .

Thoughts/Images

Fir

The fir stands.
The man watches.
Its height pierces the low cloud.
Its arms stretch out to the winds.
Its roots walk deep into the earth.
The man watches.
The fir stands.
The man walks away.
"Perhaps you are right," he says.

Balance

The saline walkers held a feast
in the gardens of honey.

And the king of bitterness
came and ruled over them.

The Respectful Thief

"Wuh," cried the thief,
leaning against the pillar
in the dark museum,

(and the colors dazzled
like a thousand eyes)

"they are as good at it
as I am . . . "

Funk

The great god Shango in the African sea
reached down with palm oil and oozed out me.

Peas

Peas in the pod
peas in my gut
peas in the belly roll
doing the strut.
Blackeyes over
blackeyes down
blackeyes browneyes going to town

Yams

I made a yamship for my belly with my spoon
and sweet riding jelly bread kept me til noon.

Fish

Catfish niggerfish
low in the creek
Catfish blackfish
none all week

baitworm doughball
put your glad rags on
hook me a catfish ninefeet tall.

niggerspit catfish bit
only was a crawdad hole

good bait sent catfish went
must be fishin the whiteman's hole

Fingers

Between the great silver veil
      of the water moon
and the thirsty hot soil
      of the earth valley,

      I touched you
      softly with
      fingers of rain.

America

If an eagle be imprisoned
On the back of a coin
And the coin is tossed into the sky,
That coin will spin,
That coin will flutter,
But the eagle will never fly.

Thought

Lord, how I wept when I came upon
a land whose people thought that they
could make boats sail the stormy
ocean between the color of my skin
and my humanity.

Thought

Love came to me and said:
What do you want of me?
Save me I said, Save me.
Love knelt down beside me
and love said:
If you knew the price
of coming to you,
you would ask nothing
but would give.

Thought

One of the greatest roles
ever created by Western man
has been the role of "Negro."

One of the greatest actors
to play the role has been
the "Nigger."

Thought

First impressions tend to direct the path
of a friendship.
That is why the black man and the white man
seldom meet.

Thought

I flew into the country of the mind
and there my wings froze.
I fell.
Thought sculptured me in stone.

Thought

"You're lying," said Memory.
"You're asleep," said Forgetfulness.

Thought

Hate is also creative:
it creates more hate.

Image

I saw
    a raindrop
            falling.
I said
    it was
        a thought
            coming
back.
    It
      hit
        me,
splattering.
      I was
          amazed.

Image

Into the dawn light
the shadow walks behind you.
Into the night
and it leads.

Image

The universe shrank
when you went away.
Everytime I thought your name,
stars fell upon me.

Image

With an eyelash
I etched your form
upon the moon.

Image

The lights gathering
on the night lake
sing a thousand songs
of the sleeping sun.

Image

The sun
bending over
the basins of my eyes
this morning
washed his hand.

Image

The high hills of hell
are low around me.

Kef (Selections)

Kef 3

The only legends that I have ever heard
about the American Southland are those
which portray it as a brute land of evil
and decay, a land uncompromising in
its attitudes toward the state of its own
human soul, a land of sordid myths and
terrifying realities. Therefore I must
go to the South to hear and see what
the truth is, for I speak as a Northerner.
If there is no good in the Southland
worth the enrichment and the fabric of
language and symbol, then I think it
time that we Americans go South and live.

Kef 4

The sacred temple of Gnosaam stands
three feet tall in the yellow sands
of al-Hajid where *schlamaal* blows
down the sky and the hammer
of the universe strikes blows
that drive the wandering tribes
of Bedu off their camels to fall

two feet off the ground crying:
Al-haam d'ullah, al-haam d'ullah.

Kef 9

Potato skin beneath my fingernail,
juice and dust.
Aching knobs growing on the balls of my knees.
I will tote potatoes in this sack.
Potato skin, sore and torn.
Dust in the morning, dust at noon.
All fill the sacks!
'Tatoes are dying in the dust.
Pull 'em out, put 'em in!
I will tote potatoes on my back.
My forehead's throbbing, my neck
is baking, every time I fall,
I sneeze.

I rather be a 'tato in the ground,
than keep on coughing and falling down.
I rather be a 'tato in the sack
than carry a 'tato on my back.

Kef 13

They sang,
Don't forget the bridge
that brought you all over!

What bridge, I asked.

Jesus is the One, they sang.
Jesus is the One that brought
you all over.

Out of the wilderness of Sin,
He brought you all over.

Where was the wilderness? I asked.

And they sang,
Don't forget the bridge
that brought you all over!
Jesus is the Bridge
that brought you all over!

Kef 27

I'm gonna go into the house
and sit at the table and eat up
everything I see, and then I gonna think about
what I ate, then I gonna get up from that table
and I gonna stretch myself a little bit and then
I'm gonna think about what I'm gonna do after that,
and then I gonna do it, and after I do it,
I'm gonna think about what I did.

Kef 54

i broke three limbs before i
swung out over the stream
and after i ran for two hours
i was very dry except that i
sweated a lot and the salt
would creep through the corners
of my mouth and i would spit
as i breathed out with my whole
body because the pressure of
my bones was driving all my
muscles up into my skull which
drifted back and forth on my
shoulders and i knew i could
not stop even though it finally
happened and i almost died to
see my skull hanging over in
front of me swinging from
side to side like a pendulum.

Kef 73

Ichneumon came knocking at my door.
He was a giant wolf with wings as wide clouds.
But he was polite,

Kef 86

Walk with your head held too high
and someone will think
you are holding your neck
out—like a stupid chicken—
to be cut off.

Kef 106

The Mosaics are a people filled with color.
They are a people born because
God is just and loves the just.
The Mosaics sing, dance, and pray in color.

Kef 107

The holidays of the Mosaics are legends of color.
Number one
is the Holy Day of Red.
Number two
is the Holy Day of Black.
Number three is the Holy Day of Green.
Number four is the Holy Day of Blue.
Number five is the Holy Day of Yellow.
Number six is the Holy Day of Blindness.

Kef 124

The green field undulated
on ribbons of colors,
and the grass people leaped up
on dandelion balloons.

An air river flowed across
the field and drowned them.
The green field banked and rose,
reaching out with wild arms,
screeching in terrified gestures
of colors:
Give me back my people
or I will swallow you up!

Kef 141

gave you my eyes
my feet
my soul
and my life
what do what what
what do want?

gave you my tongue
my heart
my veins
my voice
and all that i want
what oh what baby
what do you want?

gave you
gave you gave you
gave you
gave you
gave gave gave gave gave gave gave
and if you want
i will
give
i will give again

KEF: SECOND SERIES

Kef 2

I want some mo straawberries.
I luv straawberries.
Straawberries tastzz good.

I'm coming
down to your valley.
I will crawl on my knees in the grass.
I will finger-part the grassezz.

And then and then and then and then . . .

I will take my finger in the hand,
and I will touch the berry,
the cherry-berries,
seedy berries,
hairy berries,
bloody berries.

And then and then I will make
the little seed-wheels roll thru
out the labyrinthine rutty ridges
of the road of my tongue
flooded by my saliva sea.
Oooh . . . a goood tasting berry
which I cherry . . .
ishh-uuuuuuuuuuuuummmmmmmmmmmmmmmmmmmm . . .

Kef 6

Ego told Id to do it,
but Id didn't hear him
because he was doing it.

Kef 12

Take up the blood from the grass, sun.
Take it up.
These people do not thirst for it.
Take up the insect children that play in
the grass, sun.
Take them away.
These people are sick of them.
Take down the long slender reeds, sun.
Cut them down.
These people cannot make flutes any longer.
Now sun, come closer to the earth!
Even closer than that.
Closer. Now, sun.
Take away the shape from the metal, sun.
They are like stone, these people.
Now make them lava.

Kef 16

Down near the levee where the river once
broke through the sand and the dirt,

Down where the north fish drown in muddy
waters, where mountains become silt heaps,

I used to sit and throw out the wiggling worm,
as I dreamed of giant catfish asleep beneath

the blood.

Kef 21

First there was the earth in my mouth. It was there like
a running stream, the July fever sweating the delirium
of August, and the green buckling under the sun. The
taste of sick dust ran in the currents of saliva which I
heaved up and tried to picture when all the people
would curse their own stinking guts and die. No. I am
not wishing that everyone should die. Nor am I wishing
that everyone should be still. Only I am squeezing out
the steam in me.

Kef 22

there they go
the lips
slipping and sliding
there they go
the hips
ripping and riding
there there
and where does the river end
the red nose of the sun
sun
sucks the sand blows at the mouth
of the sea of time

men
drunk on the falling sky
wet with the sweet brine
and the sea which never lies
hail
I hail three ships
our bodies breaking the waves
there they go
the dips and rises
hail
i hail thee
death and

Kef 24

lay sixteen bales down in front on the plank
let me set and bay at the houndog moon
lay sixteen bales down of the cotton flank
pray with me brothers that the pink
boss dont sweat me too soon
beat my leg in a round nigger peg
lord have mercy on my black pole
lay sixteen bales in the even row
let me sweat and cuss my roustabout tune
lord have mercy on my shrinkin back
let me go with the jesus mule
lay sixteen bales for the warp and loom
beat a nigger down and bury his soul
boss dont sweat me too soon
pray with me brothers that I hold my cool
lord have mercy on this long black leg
let me ride on the jesus mule
lay sixteen bales of white fuzz down

lay sixteen tales of how I got around
lord have mercy on this sweat and stink
lord have mercy
lay sixteen bales
pray brothers
beat down
lord have
let me
lord lord
brothers
the houndog moon
howl jesus,
howl!

Kef 25

the swan silvertone singers
pulled chords of blue and purple
like the velvet robe of king Nkoko
sounding in their sounding
of gut and Benin strut
paying no mind to the bean
and unseen mama walkers and owl
talkers laying it up close
to the night pose perching
peeking seeing
all the silvermoon lies of throat
and tongue splitting
in the unknown

Kef 30

high and up high
low and below
between neon domes
and silicon smoke sooting,
flew the eagle,
the raped dove dripping
baptismal wine,
and in america the grand
canyon is filled with blood

it is the biggest cup in the world
waiting for the biggest cannibal
in the world to grow very very hungry

Kef 31

my head is over
there
looking with my eyes over
here
the wind in the crevices of my skull
brings news from far cities
long leveled
on the edge of a distant Egypt
broken in colors
near the brain
which sucks my eyes back
and I think I am sleeping now

Kef 32

The night is one wing
the day the other
and he balances both
on ozone and uses my
thought for bone.

Kef 33

of late i have caved into myself
searching with daydimmed eyes
the musty catacombs of mind
tunneling finally
into bone which leads outside

Kef 35

gimme somo dat
gimme somo dat
gimmesomodat
n den n den he tuk me up
n as i was layin there he tuk me down
n he say like he hear me say in de first
gimme somo dat
das good?
he say
das gimme somo dat good now gimme oo

Kef 39

for thirty one pieces of silver
thats right baby
we live in the modelled age
you take a man's coat
before you take his throat
the price is up
we atomize everything baby,
atomisize, thirty one

Kef 40

the united hates of america:
when the pilgrim fathers on the goodship
jesus, brought 20 negars from
africa, they learned to live with them-
selves by hating
their love of god who was jesus three
times, and in my hunger
they failed to ask my name,
and called me negro, and united
now under one banner, we the 20 million
bibleleaf eating cannibals are eager
to eat again, and this time we want
meat for strength. We have a journey
to take and little time;
we have ships to name
and crews.

Kef 43

we shall be climbing over that wall
tonite
when sentry eyes blink
we shall (tell Kaksi and Mleybla
           send no drummers yet
           build no fires yet
           drink no water yet
           kill no wandering flies
           wait for the sign
           of the split hoof)
we shall be
           (tell
           —speak clearly fool
           your dribble is drowning
           the feet of your words—
           Jimmy and Willy
           blow no horn yet
           raise no flag yet
           buy no car yet
           wait for the sign
           of the flying red horse
           to fall, then we ride)

           stand on the brink
flinging Zeus for Jesus
singing new notes every target made.

Kef 44

Off the coast of Spain
down near Gibraltar, there is a place

called Tarifa, and Tarifa
the wind blows up against your body
and you cannot fall down against it
and you just keep leaning on it if you wish
and then it gets into your skin and wears it
and it cuts years in lines on your face before
you have the years really in Tarifa.
I shall fly to this place and lean . . .

Kef 45

nighthawk of time
what message see you over these barren
termite tunnels of brick and metro steel?

the tolling of the Empire bell
signals the mad rush
down the corridors of hell

nighthawk of time
you saw the redman in the belly
of the buffalo
tell me nighthawk of day what does it mean?

they will come tomorrow and ask me why the bell
clanks instead of tolling and I will say
learning has not been a process with me

nighthawk of the tolling bells spiral
wings over the streetlamp night of branch
and moth hushing

tell me of the bituminous rock and painted earth
dry beneath your circling vision

I hear the sequoia and the redwood bend when
you bend, come back, then
fall, arrow!

the tolling of the inner skull ringing
some litany down from eclipsed sky
blackwhite tipped lightning wing!

I speak with unknown tongues and clefs
screaming Iuna in the corridors

sixlegs with wings inching white up my thigh
nighthawk of the centuries

afrikan lance striking skull where grass
blades out eyes and tongues are meat
for beetles learning to read the bill
of rights
in the night without the gong of temple
shaking Christ upon the bow and arrow

I speak with the beak split in the scream
of dream of tolling bells

over the ruins of trampled mudhuts and wire
tents, what see you bird?

what feel you breast on the belly of america?
feather me back past the isle of crows and mice
past the sale of tribe
past the infinite toll of God beating
his wings
rising up to
dine
on us?

Kef 57

Kale rocks in the black
boat-skillet of grease
and boiling water and
soon the fork impales
the green leaves up
and the mouth-bridge opens.

IKEFS (IKONS OF KEF)

Ikef 4

when we needed rain
dust came
out in that far lagoon
when we threw nets
fish fled
when i wept in the bed
of your shadow
tears drowned me

we are the thin-ribbed
people
begging bread and fish
from the wind

even the rocks weep
salt for us

Ikef 5: Children Playing

like small trees
we hid in the grass

straight was the shadow
beside

birds like voices
finding us

calling the wind
to stroke our backs

bending we know
the brown tongue
of this grass

sharp words tell

hurry they will see us

Ikef 9: Black Widow

red is the hour glass
(who will mark the
widow's time?)

she scuttles across
her ruses

What shall he bring
her?

red is the cup
And who sent the
nigger wandering in
the night?

Come back.
Your blood is not
     theirs . . .

Look at my watch.

Ikef 10

They cry "Revolution!"
jamming charred sticks
at the stuffed heads
of strawmen
     leaning and broken
     by the wind.

I recall days of my running
with willow lances
beating
the American skies . . .

At dusk
children must retire
     behind the
          sun.

Ikef 11

In the green black
paradise of Obi
and Mtu
we heard the howl

of wolves come
over the sea from
the cold north.

The palm-wine
and the drum received
the music played upon
harps of ice.

And we heard what we
did not hear,
(we Egyptian priests
    digging in the belly of
    mothers) and lo
    the wolf-ships rock
off shore, ready to rape . . .

Ikef 13

Cawing
some tune remembered
in his nest
the crow
shit on my head.

If it had been the eagle
I would have grown angry.

But it was the gnawing
bird.

When will we cease
bowing?

Ikef 16: Guts

1—Into the kaleidoscopic bowl of Harlem
   I stuck my good fingers
   (remembering the frost-bitten days
   of cleaning the labyrinths of chitterlings)

   and the bite of the niggerfish
   struck the bowl red.
2—Black sharks,
   we are shackled in white foam.

3—Is there no smell sweeter than our own blood?

4—Ah, here the story of the shark:
   eating with glass teeth black images

5—I too scream when I weep.

6—Return to your teacher beyond the neon bowl.
   To the sea!
   To the sea!

7—Even sharks . . .

Ikef 18: Breathe with Me

"When I cry," said the mountain,
"two streams meet me yonder."

"Yes, I know," said the sky.

"And when I laugh," said the mountain,
"it is the same joy."

"Two streams?"

"Yes."

"Which have become my great mirror,"
said the sky. "Come,

Breathe with me."

Ikef 20: Soil

Things fell from the trees after
the rain.

All that glass money.

Somebody's got a lot to pay back.

Ikef 21: A Long Time Coming

Snow, like lost cotton heads in the wind,
blanketed us.
It came (as we) from a long shape over that
hill
to settle
(ah, a person can die waiting to freeze)
under the wind
a long time coming
                    and coming

Saba (Selections)

Saba

there are maggots in my corn
i have no command of flies

nor do the maggots cease their chewing
i have no command of flies

the pastor came yesterday
"a man born of the spirit," he said

"sows and reaps."
i told him i had no command of flies

the root doctor came today
with a dark bottle of dances

shaking his gnarled fist at the sky
leaving me no command of flies

tomorrow a planter will inspect my corn
for the factory which

has no command of flies

Saba: The Lost Diadem

gold like buried lances from the sun
used to leap up from the rocks when he walked
        where is our king?
        fossilized in our brains
        waiting for a golden crown
african sons flailing at history, digging
up our fathers and weeping for the rains

Saba: Shadow and Act

a black shadow limped behind the blond king
making an invisible rope from shreds of blood
a shadow grows blacker and taller as the sun sets
(this aint no big thing but its all we got)
with a flip of his whip the king permits the moon
growing out of the darkness the black man counts
the stars, tightens his rope, and pulls them down

Saba: Black Paladins

we shall be riding dragons in those days
black unicorns challenging the eagle
        we shall shoot words
        with hooves that kick clouds
        fire eaters from the sun
we shall lay the high white dome to siege
cover screams with holy wings, in those days
                we shall be terrible

Saba

The word shall descend
    upon us
before we learn to speak
    and it shall
stop us before we break

Saba

all the letters i have written you
(an empty hall of echoes)
swirl where the wind has left them

i am learning/the alphabet/of the wind

footsteps . . .

Saba

i am taking pictures over this bridge
           between us
first picture: iris of August bowing
second picture: i make a rainbow
third picture: i can actually see you
fourth picture: hooped in my wheel
fifth picture: rolling towards March

sixth picture: ice snowing the ridge
seventh picture: i waited for you
eighth picture: this boy believed

ninth picture: his shadow would answer
tenth: can i see when i close my eye?
eleventh: i caught you forgetting me
twelfth: negative: between us, a shutter

Saba

we were piling feathers on a long plain
playing yesterdays
clouds of falling birds

let us not revive the sun dead behind
yesterday's nest

what we built in laughter under the wind
is captured forever on each feather

Saba

statues do not feel like that
sun like ultraviolet eels
shimmering over your skin

i am catching my shadow like that
the falling of forms
is light making fantasies

of my statue ramming (whose

skin burns designs forgotten
streaming yes it heals
billowing shadows of brown skins

jamming the world inside out)

Saba

i lay in the gutter
i like gin
it looks like glass
in golden

i hear the silver swan
tell Zeus i have caught
Pegasus to ride inside

Saba Tam Fiofori

sea earth
sea above earth
strike
sea that breaks

sailing never stops
waves blue to sever
shake this sea til sources

Saba

Tao was the first priest
and he (with Yret, the second)
came unto God
and Tao said:

You are wasting your talents
Yret nodded his heavy head
Tao sat down upon the throne of God

God, who had drawn the curtain
over his vision when he first saw them,
watched their shadows from
the garden
(a green garden of snakes and streams)

Saba of the Snow and the Sun

your eyes made the bridge of our existence
a snow flake aching to attack the sun
the rivers of the sun flood
death is light and shadows of flesh
darkness is sight upon your space
i am touching
cold wings flying cold wings flaking

i would not slide into you less i slide
banks receiving the burn of blood
death is life: flowers
i am you are we were the now and now
nor have i nor snow without water

the sun is black
your sighs made the signs of our insistence

Shaba

1

trembling valleys making tongues of air
jetting up your deep breath
(i shall take a dive into the Msippi
where the trembling thighs fell
anticipating the sea)

i am setting up a line with hooks
trembling in the fierce mother wind
you dance up

and i shall go fishing in my dark well
rippling under your deep breath
(i shall fish along these abandoned
shores hearing your song)

i shall give birth
trembling in your soulwind and
i will know the inhabitants of this sea

2

she was a fighter with shreds of flesh
beneath her nails
light would break upon her face
and call her smile a song of war
she was a lone island

Saba

we weep that our heroes have died
in our memories
our historians and preachers
remind us that we had warriors
who fought the boot of the devils
who came in Jesus ships from Europe

we weep that our forefathers kneeled
and let the knife take our tongues

we weep that no one weeps for us
what is this?
are we what we are?
listen! we are not what we will be
what is this weeping and screaming?

a people cannot create the real hero
until they create the real hero
not by mirrors or masks or muscles
but by men the soil is nourished
and one day
we will not weep but sing him
up

Saba   Out

sx waterings
        streams
striking aorta
         vibraphones

134

sx veinings
       myriads
of flagella flucksing rite

   Saba

we shall be baking stones upon the mesa
cold rain speaking up from faces sweet-shadowed
(et toro)
there are no reaping farmers to talk to grass

who will hunt with us upon the sky of rocks
to reach ice and
break stones into black blood buried under sun?

   Saba   In

within the wailing
soon lines stagger
god is a drunk fisherman
    one snake
worming the world
within
working up oldmen's tales of me

   Saba   Saba

sound sets up music for the skeleton
and sound
gathers: i am gettingtogetherherenow

and sound begets models
which sail for pirates against pirates

listen
sound senses sayings even i intend

to gather shadows nodding in my palm
you are an unbated tickler of lice
if you have not swum in the calm
and the shaking body of this ocean

resounding ever over sense and form
which breaks ships
to make them again on screaming waves

Saba

kite string
wordless tongue
caught by fierce winds

chord embryonic
dried blood
i do not try to drink of the sea anymore

no kite but a string of . . .

Saba

no this dream was not like a penny
shining in

the hippos of the mud
swallow my directions

no this dream was not like any
what all you people doing in here
(i am the mud slinger on your back)

they—(see this jello seem?—
walk from high to low)

atavistic images on a spinning coin
step out
no this seems

Jonah upon a dry land is stumbling
broken-necked into my reflections

Saba

the hand that
lovely womanish
the web caps the skull
touches once prints

so soon i am young again
then points
old woman i love your babe

Saba: Joy

purchase two
eat one
and
give the other away

Songthesis:
East St. Louis
Epiphanies

The sun is shining arrows

Epiphany

(to Eugene Redmond)

A man runs out into a field.
The sun is shining arrows.
The rivers of the earth
converge and fan out from
his feet and the mountains
east of the moon and west
of everything else
grow beneath his feet
and all the clothed
and feathered birds
watch him from the road
and the man takes off
joyously all
his clothes!

East Saint Hell

(Up from the Ghetto)

RECALL!

They shall come to you one day
and they shall laugh and say,
Tell us again the place you come from.

Do not laugh with them or at them,
but rather recall—
in the simmering urn of your mind—
the stench clinging to your child feet
and the glorious time of cleaning
up the stench—pine perfume and smiles—

recall the cracking of your father's bones
when he went down under the night stick
and rose up again with Jesus's cross,
an axe-club drawing blood in his fisthand

recall the hunger rat ulcering through
the plate of your stomach
and the rent worm inching up your mama's leg

recall the days when you shut your eyes
so tight to see beyond it all

that the ceiling fell and the wintertime
of the hawk became your bed of bones

so tight that your brother died
in a pool of frozen blood outside the bank
recall those days,
your eyes,
so tight
that stars became your eyes and you
could see deep into the night
and see without sight,

recall the stars falling in your lap
at your feet
Great sparkling rug-robe trailing

recall your hammerheaded tears
bombing the terrain of desires

recall that urge coming on
the plain of the ghetto
leaping madmen with fires

recall your eyes firebombing
the July skies

recall the hearse of ashes
like the beetle of death
scuttling through a world of shit

Yes, do not laugh at them,
and do not laugh with them
but just recall that rhythm of flesh
drumming up your words

recall the color of your black blood
spreading out
the delta voice of the Mississippi
recall your sweet blood tearing
the earth

and recall then the voice
your mother and your father
singing

recall, and when they come to you
one day and say
tell us again the place you come from,

say to them
Where I come from is where you are going

A Rainbow Around the Neck of Night

from your face where night sleeps
strain was my mirror of pain
and this is my red blood
leaping up like meteors gone mad

come, pretty necklace in black
i will make you queen
of my crown under the sun

Owed to Otis

(after Eugene Redmond's "Still Soaring Black Angel")

I saw the iron wings
fold around him and the plane
crashed . . .
But his wings were fashioned
from spiritual voodoo
his bones
filled with the air of his songs

And when I hear the shout
of James Brown
I see the red wings of Otis
flying higher and higher!
and when Wilson picks up the
chant
I see the red wings flying higher
higher!
When Ray charms the wild air
I see the red wings higher!
and higher!
when Sam tells Dave
then I rave
higher higher!

Brown Sound

brown sound chocolate
memories
like the first time
you saw grapes
and tasted them
and learned the color
blue

brown sound cream milk
echoes
like the first time
you saw bees
and tasted gold
and learned the honey
tongue

brown sound africa
pulses
like the first time
you exploded between legs
and heard drums
and learned the message
of rhythm love

brown sound america
pulses plus pushing
down trees
like the first time
you saw that wild crazy horse
riding through painted deserts
and you learned the grand canyon
red mother

brown sound
black outline
like the first time
like the first time
the first time
is the last time
like that

Greatness

each man-string
doing his own thing
vibrating at the

each-to-each volume
sounding at the
each-to-each pitch
all being heard
at the same time
no one pushing
no one behind
each knowing each's
rhythm and sign

each man
a string on the harp
doing its own destiny
no one pushing
no one behind
each man
the end
and the beginning
of harmony

Beyond Selves

How did I come to see myself in the mirror?
Wearing clothes I saw the clothes
Wearing worn smiles I saw laughter, not tears
Wearing frowns I felt pain not suffering
How does a soul begin to know its own image?
By turning around and looking at the world?
No.
By stripping in front of the mirror
with your eyes closed.

Don't Be Too Sure

For many nights I heard singing
and saw fireflies
camping in the forests.

One nite the wind blew winged lights
vibrating into my yard
and into my hand

That is the night I discovered
another species of firefly.
Unlike the first in every way.

He did not sing but crawled up
my leg like a tiny tank
and devoured the first in my hand.

"to meet the lord . . ."

to meet the lord of the Forests
pan
All
black
pan napping napping

even horns wake us and break us
cake us together again and brake us

pat us together again in the pan
all hands clapping
all handsclapping
awake along zambesi falls into
our lake in America
the Mississippi the runaway lake
toward the forests
toward the wild new *Forest Flowers*

come! all you forest people
come
let us name trees again
and rocks
and rivers
and creeping things
flying morning wings
let us name ourselves
the people of the sun
the people of the sun
the people of the sun

Kef 35

you shouldn't have to re sing
you shouldn't have to re write anything
you shouldn't have to re write anything
you shouldn't have to back out of a ditch
if you were headed in the right direction
if you were driving straight
in the path
not drunk but *high* up in the seat to see

you shouldn't have to re make a baby
you shouldn't have to break in the door
if the thresh and thrash fresh and flesh
and fresh threshold knows the leather of
your feet and licks the bottom soles
you shouldn't have to re make a baby
because you can't

you shouldn't have to
re create
you shouldn't have to
recreate what you create
create
beeeee!

you don't have to see anything
except what you see
created
deep inside
out your widening eyes
creating
CRE   EATING!

Songthesis

(for Sue Dlugo)

At his ear a great pearl conch.
            In front of children he passes
on the singing beach
            balancing the sun.

Across a yellow plain
            he embraces
a city of stone and steel.

Nodding at his discoveries
            he watches the moon
bathe in the bowl
            and he hears her whisper,
"What are you making in the bowl?"

His ears wing
            eastward . . . bird eggs
slumbering.

Wild horses wake him
            stammering
and she asks,
"What are you baking in the bowl?"

At his ear the humming bird.
            In back of time he traces

nuances, smiles, and shooting stars!
              that leave him blind with
eyes . . . libido torches.
              "What are you shaking
in the bowl?"

She asks him inside echoes
              through forests
of oceanic rain (he hears
      somebody's wind roaring).
Churning and churning, he breathes,
              "This is the way
              I make
              poems."

A New Proposal

(to my wife after literal kef)

i will go with you again to the field
to pick wild roses

and skip flatround stones off the lake
up and into the sky

(a rocked fanged hillside
driving us stumbling home thru the storm)

i will gather our roseseeds together with you
again and plant them in due sun

and handle their tender growth with care-
ful fingers

This is because i see you coming lovely
as i crawl from my hangover after sleep.

Your pace—even and steady I am risen
to your coming form.

As we balance the road together,
dont stop running if you dont see me
ahead sometimes because,

i never forget the scent of wild roses
and i still see how we used to sail into the sky.

About Henry Dumas

Born on July 20, 1934, in Sweet Home, Arkansas, Henry Lee Dumas packed his brief life with potent poetry, fables, vignettes, literary and social activism, teaching, varied travels, enduring friendships and illuminating experiences before he was killed suddenly—and mysteriously—by a New York City Transit policeman, in the subway, on May 23, 1968. Notable among his experiences and travels were his upbringing in Harlem, graduation from Commerce High School, study at City College of New York, a stint in the U.S. Air Force, more study at Rutgers, marriage and two sons—David and Michael, and work as a developer of little magazines: *Umbra, Camel, American Weave, Untitled, Hiram Poetry Review, Negro Digest, Collection.* These experiences also included Civil Rights activism, Hiram College Upward Bound, the Black Arts Circuit and Southern Illinois University's Experiment in Higher Education in East St. Louis, where he spent 1967-68 as a teacher-counselor and director of language workshops. The "cult" of Henry Dumas has emerged and mushroomed since his death and with the publication of five volumes of his stories and poems—*Play Ebony Play Ivory, Ark of Bones, Jonoah and the Green Stone, Rope of Wind,* and *Goodbye, Sweetwater.*

During the 1970s celebrations of Dumas' work garnered standing-room-only audiences at places like the Inner City Cultural Center in Los Angeles, the Rainbow Sign in Berkeley, California State University in Sacramento, Kuumba Workshop in Chicago, Southern Illinois University in East St. Louis, Howard University in Washington D.C., and the United Nations's International House in New York City.

Last year, with the publication of *Goodbye, Sweetwater,* cultural-literary luminaries like Avery Brooks, Raymond Patterson, Imamu Amiri Baraka, Toni Morrison, the Paul Robeson Jazz Group, Jayne Cortez, Xam Wilson Cartier, and Leo Chears have spearheaded Dumas celebrations at the Schomburg Center for Research in Black Culture in Harlem, Guild Books in Chicago, and East St. Louis's City Centre.

In Summer of 1988 a special edition of *Black American Literature Forum* was published. It contained work on Henry Dumas by several dozen leading writers and critics, including Maya Angelou, Quincy Troupe, John A. Williams, Arnold Rampersad, Toni Morrison, Gwendolyn Brooks, Ishmael Reed, Imamu Amiri Baraka, Margaret Walker, and Clyde Taylor.

Henry Dumas's widow, Loretta Dumas, and son, Michael, live in Somerset, New Jersey, where Mrs. Dumas is a staff member of the Mason Gross School of the Arts at Rutgers University.

—E.B.R.

153

About Eugene B. Redmond

As literary executor of the Henry Dumas Estate, Eugene B. Redmond has edited six volumes of the late writer's works and a special Summer 1988 Dumas Issue of *Black American Literature Forum*. Redmond has also edited or written nine other collections of poetry, fiction, and literary criticism, and has been Writer-in-Residence at California State University/Sacramento, the University of Missouri/St. Louis, Oberlin College, the University of Lagos in Nigeria, Southern University in Baton Rouge, and the University of Wisconsin/Madison. In 1976, his native city of East St. Louis, Illinois named him Poet Laureate. During the Winter 1989 semester, Redmond served as Distinguished Visiting Professor of Afro-American Studies and English at Wayne State University in Detroit. He is also Poetry Editor of the new magazine *Literati Chicago*.